I0129159

Francis Taylor Piggot, Thomas Lea Southgate

The Music and Musical Instruments of Japan

Francis Taylor Piggot, Thomas Lea Southgate

The Music and Musical Instruments of Japan

ISBN/EAN: 9783744662598

Printed in Europe, USA, Canada, Australia, Japan

Cover: Foto ©Thomas Meinert / pixelio.de

More available books at **www.hansebooks.com**

THE MUSIC

AND

MUSICAL INSTRUMENTS

OF

JAPAN.

BY

F. T. PIGGOTT.

(WITH *NOTES* BY T. L. SOUTHGATE.)

LONDON :

B. T. BATSFORD, 94, HIGH HOLBORN.

1893.

LONDON :

PRINTED BY WILLIAM CLOWES AND SONS, LIMITED,
STAMFORD STREET AND CHARING CROSS.

敬る
此書を寄る
師友なる
前田夫人へ
奉る

TO MY

FRIEND AND TEACHER

MRS MAËDA

ANY Preface which I write to the following pages must of necessity be so full of apologies for their shortcomings that I shall reduce it to the smallest compass possible.

The book contains the results of observations made in leisure moments in Japan, supplemented by studies made since my return from the East. I am now painfully conscious how incomplete those observations must have been. I have, nevertheless, some confidence in the accuracy of the results of my Western studies, because I have had more than an author's fair share of assistance from others more competent than I to grapple with scientific difficulties.

Sir John Stainer has, with customary kindness, helped me to unravel some of the mysteries of the Japanese scale : and, though I have no right to say that my conclusions are justified by his assent to them, I may plead his help to show that they have not been lightly arrived at.

Mr. Southgate's erudition and historical knowledge have been placed so unreservedly at my disposal that I cannot but regret that the sheaf of notes with which he has contented himself is of such modest proportions.

b

Finally, Mr. Daigoro Goh with Eastern patience, has pruned away many—I hope all—of the errors in names, dates, and words which so easily beset the Western writer on Eastern things.

I have made use of the following authorities :—

> *Sōkyoku-tai-i Shō*, by Yamada Ryū, 1781.
> *Miyako-no-nishiki*, by Miyakoji Bungo, 1785.
> *Seikyoku Ruizan*, by Saitō Gekkin, 1840.
> *Kabu-Ongaku Ryakushi*, by Professor Konakamura, 1887.
> "MS. Records of Ancient Music," by Abé Suyenao.
> The Encyclopædia, *Sansai Zuyé.*
> *Honchō Seidan* by Kikuoka Senryō.
> "La Musique du Japon," by M. Alexandre Kraus Fils.

The translations in Japan have all been made by Mr. A. T. Kawaji, of Tokyo, who has also interpreted a great number of conversations with various musicians. Mr. Kowaki has assisted me with many translations in England.

Of the book itself I have but one word to say. It appeared in its earliest form as a Paper read before the Asiatic Society of Japan, in January, 1891 I have endeavoured to remove many errors which existed in that Paper In its present form it is a contribution, *quantum valeat*, to the history of the music and musical instruments of the world. Among the things which go to make it up, some, I hope, may be of interest : some may be merely curious : and some, I venture to think, will be surprising.

                                                         F. T. P.

May, 1893.

TABLE OF CONTENTS.

PART I.

THE MUSIC OF THE JAPANESE.

PART II.

THE JAPANESE SCALE.

PART III.

THE MUSICAL INSTRUMENTS OF THE JAPANESE.

LIST OF PLATES.

—·••◦••◦·—

LIST OF ILLUSTRATIONS.

THE MUSIC OF THE JAPANESE.

PROPERTY OF THE
CITY OF NEW YORK

THE

MUSIC OF THE JAPANESE.

"Harmony has the power to draw Heaven downwards to the Earth. It inspires men to love the good, and to do their duty. If one should desire to know whether a kingdom is well governed, if its morals are good or bad, the quality of its Music shall furnish forth the answers."—CONFUCIUS.

SYNOPSIS.

Of the teaching of Confucius, and the meaning of "music" in the Far East — Of modern Japanese music and instruments generally — The mythology of Japanese music: how Amaterasu was enticed from her cave: of the invention of the Koto and Flute of Japan: of the influence of the Hichiriki: traces of early music — Early historical records: the teaching of the Corean musicians: the zeal of the Crown Prince Umayado—The establishment of Chinese music in Japan: the Musical Bureau: the development of the Bugaku dances—Lingering traces of the old music of Japan: primitive sacred music: of the Kagura, and its modern offshoots—Early forms of Japanese music: the Ro-yei, and the Ima yô.—Introduction of the Biwa: the Satsuma Biwa: of the Heiké Monogatari.— Influence of the Biwa on the national music: the Saiba-gaku, and the Dengaku.— The Chinese and Japanese dances: the "Nô" dances. — The early Japanese Theatre — Early Japanese songs: their classification: the Joruri Mono-gatari—[A scheme of Chinese and Japanese dances and music—A scheme

IF I say that Japanese music does not lack some reflex of the national
grace, that it has some prettily quaint flashes of melody which strike
the most inattentive listener at a tea-house festival, that it has some curious
phrase-repetitions which seem to the attentive listener to indicate the
possible existence of a science of construction, and that generally it is not
altogether a concourse of weird sounds, it will appear to many that I have
not merely stated, but have overstated, the case in its favour.

From our Western point of view Japanese music has everything against
it, nothing in its favour: we with our majestic Organs, our stupendous orchestras, our volumes of sound, which set the nerves, even of the unmusical,
quivering: they with a few pitiful strings strung by men not very learned
in the mysteries of sound-producing bodies, the subtleties of varnish, the pre-
cedents of "bellies." Comparison is absurd: the tinkling of their Samisens
hardly reaches ears accustomed to sonorous symphonies from earliest infancy.[1]
Their appliances are so crude: how, with instruments so feeble, can they
make that music which beats upon the brain, which so plays on the nervous

tissues that their vibrations fill the caverns of the memory with whispering voices of the past? How, indeed! The quality of music is so often lost in the quality of the sound which makes it. It is the noise and blare of great Organs that have brought to Western music, perhaps also to Western religions, half their devotees. It is the witchery of the fiddle and the bow that holds two-thirds of a London audience in their places. Rob the high art of music of its attendant mysteries of sound, what is left concerns the musician alone, and with his joy few of the outer barbarians can intermingle. The "Hallelujah Chorus" on two Flutes (it was once, as I have heard, so "arranged"), "Pop goes the Weasel," with variations and orchestral accompaniments—is there much doubt which would command the larger audience? And yet the childish frivolity of "Up and down the City Road" would be unaltered, and that wonderful phrase, "For the Lord God omnipotent reigneth," would still remain the most fitting expression of a majestic thought.

What Japanese music might have been if the Shō, the primeval Organ, had amplified its soft reeds in the East instead of in the West; whether the "missing notes" would have been so deliberately disregarded as, in the popular music, they seem to have been; whether their use would not have taught a larger science and more sweet melody, it is scarcely profitable to enquire; we should be led inevitably to the larger question whether, had these things been, the Japanese life, and above all the Japanese religion, would have been quite what they are. The Chinese had been taught by their great philosopher the true relation of music to life. Pope only caught half the teaching of Confucius when he sang of order as "Heaven's first law": in full it ran, and runs thus—"There are two important things which should exist in a well-ordered society: *rei*, ceremonial, order; and *gaku*, music." And the character for *gaku*, music, is the same as the character for *raku*, pleasure : whence music came to be not only synonymous with the giving of pleasure to everybody, but its influence was held in Chinese philosophy to be the chief corrective to undue and ill-regulated pleasures. It was but a step from this to the consideration of music as the divine pleasure, God-given, for the purification of the human heart. So, to the popular and largest of the Chinese stringed instruments was given a character 琴, *kin*, which had the same sound as 禁, *kin*, "prohibition"; and thence, at first, they wove the idea that its music symbolised the prohibition of anything impure, until at length "music" came to be actually synonymous with "purity of the human heart."

The Japanese, when the time came for christening as their own the *Kin* which they had borrowed from China, chose for it a name, *Koto*, to which, though it signified merely "things," they were able to attach an idea of something higher than worldly things by imagining it to be an abbreviation only, of *kami no nori koto*—"the oracles of the gods," "the heavenly things"—and hence they, in their turn, came to see in Koto music, something supernal ; and in Koto playing something synonymous with worship and invocation of the divine advice.

On its more sublunary influence, its power to subdue not animals merely, but the lower man, Eastern writers love to dwell, proving their position by the chapter and verse of recorded incident. As Congreve wrote that Music's charms can soothe savage breasts, so the Eastern poet wrote that Music can soften the thoughts even of a stern man. So let it be noted that how dissimilar soever the sounds of the East and the West may be, there is a link between them, riveted somewhere on to the heart of man.

Let us deal then with the music of this far-oriental people such as we find it. I feel, however, both considerable difficulty and diffidence in laying the results of my investigations before my readers. An opinion, which I do in fact hold, that the case in favour of Japanese music may be put much higher than I have ventured to do in my first sentence, should, for full weight to be given to it, be supported by a far wider range of examples than it is possible to give at present. The only completeness at which it was possible to aim was in the investigation of the rudiments. To the many beauties, and to the great merit, of the structure which has been raised upon them, only my own ears can bear witness.

The difficulties which stand in the way of reducing the music into Western written forms are so great, that, unless Japanese musicians will come and play to us here in England, accurate knowledge of their art, due appreciation of their craft, can only come into being in the West very gradually. If the conclusions at which I have arrived are sound, we may look, sooner or later, to have accurate transcriptions which shall lead to fuller knowledge : and I may venture so far as to say that that fuller knowledge will justify and repay the labour spent upon its acquisition. Yet we shall never hear it at its best until the deft fingers of the native musicians weave their spells for us. Much of the charm of the music, all its individuality nearly, depend upon its graceful and delicate phrasing : and though I think that Western notation is capable of expressing these phrases to one who has already heard them, I feel a little uncertain whether their more complicated forms could be set down in it with sufficient accuracy to enable a stranger to interpret them satisfactorily. The Japanese musician learns this phrasing by ear ; by an ear long trained to phrases of a similar character. My own experience has been that even in the first-grade tunes it required twenty or thirty lessons to enable one to grasp the delicate *nuances* of many of the passages.[2]

Modern Japanese music, a term to be explained more fully hereafter, is composed almost exclusively for the 13-stringed Koto.   For the Kokyu, or Fiddle, I have not come across any independent music : but for the Samisen—irreverently called by some the Banjo of Japan, an instrument with which it has no affinities—there exists a small repertoire of songs.   For the Shakuhachi—a lipped bamboo pipe—there is also a considerable quantity of independent music, which seems to have come down to the present time from quite different sources than those from which the Koto music has been derived.   The music for the Biwa has not altered for over six hundred years. The charming little songs sung to the accompaniment of the Gekkin are, I think, almost entirely of Chinese origin.

Koto music is written.   It has been many times stated that there is no notation : but the music is so complicated that it would pass the wit of man to do without some form of musical writing.   The error, however, is perhaps not to be wondered at ; it has arisen from two causes.   In the first place the books are never used except for reference : by the majority of professional musicians indeed they could not be used, for they are blind, music being one of the recognized professions of the blind.   And secondly, the written music is the exclusive possession of the professionals of the highest rank. Except by very special dispensation no pupil is ever allowed to learn in any other way than by listening, watching, and committing to memory. Hence a curious little social custom has arisen : it is considered quite im-polite for a guest to require pressing if she is asked to play the Koto : she cannot have forgotten to bring music which she never possessed.

The Samisen songs, on the other hand, are written and carried with the instrument in its case.

The Koto notation, which I shall explain in due course, is simple but sufficient; the numbers of the strings only being given. On account of the gaps in our diatonic scale which exist in the normal tuning of the instrument, I think it is easier for Europeans to learn the Koto by adopting this notation, translating the Japanese numerals into Arabic, than by writing out the melodies on a stave. Yet even for a European, more curious to know and understand than to play, the rigid rule I have referred to above will not be relaxed until he has made considerable progress. The books will remain sealed even to him : if he wants to write the tunes down he must do it for himself and invent some system of notation of his own.[3]

I have indicated briefly the different kinds of music now existing in Japan. There is one other, which is not less interesting than the rest : the ancient form of it, which, chiefly as an accompaniment to the various styles of classical dance, has been preserved for centuries, and which is still per-formed with the same profound solemnity as in old days. Such purity could only have been achieved by the Japanese method, which obtains in everything, of making the profession hereditary, and thus keeping the scores and the traditions in certain families.

Performed by an orchestra of Shōs, Flutes, Hichirikis, Drums, and Gongs, this ancient music it is which sounds so gruesome to Western ears, and to which Japanese music owes much of its bad reputation.

It is far, however, from being formless and void. It has a venerable history, which goes back through the period of reliable chronicles into the mythical ages, when the Sun-Goddess Amaterasu hid herself in a cave and

the world saw the light of her countenance no more. Then it was that the
eight million deities came to entreat her return to the world, her fair
dominion : yet all their many prayers failed, until one God, wiser than his
fellows, took from among them six long-bows ; these he bound firmly
together, and, setting them with their backs upon the ground, gently twanged

The Mythology of Japanese Music. their strings. Then he brought to the cave's mouth the fair
Amé-no-Uzumé, her hair tied with the trailing vines of *Hikage-
kazura,* gathered from the mount *Amé no Kaga Yama,* the sleeves of her
raiment girded with links of evergreen twigs of *Amé no masaki,* a halberd
in one hand and a bundle of bamboo branches in the other. And Amé-
no-Uzumé, as the murmurings of the bow-strings rose and fell, waved her
bamboo branches to and fro ; and as the rhythm grew her body moved
in cadence, and her voice mingled with the strains, until the Goddess,
gently drawn, inquisitive, came forth at last from out the gloomy
depths of her cave. Some say that Amé-no-Uzumé added to her
incantation the words *"Momo, chi, yorodsu,"* asking the Gods, in her vanity,
whether her charms were not all-potent ; the Gods shook the heavens
with their mirth, and this noise it was that drew the Goddess from her
hiding-place. Thus was light restored to the world, and music and dancing
were given to it for its delight. And the all-wise Gods had taken pre-
cautions that the light, if it should be restored, should never again be
hidden. Amatsumora, the ironsmith, had made a magic mirror, emblem of
all purity, and it was hung at the entrance to the cave. The Goddess could
never hide that face again which she then saw for the first time in all its
radiant splendour.

Tradition holds that these were the very words of the incantation :—

Hito, futa, miyo,   Gods, behold the cavern's mouth,
Itsu, muyu, nana,   Comes thence the majestic Goddess; Rejoice!
Ya, kokono, tari,   Shall not joy now fill all our hearts?
Momo, chi, yorodzu.   Are not my charms all-powerful?

In more prosaic fashion, and with *miyo* divided, this gives the numerals—

One, two, three, four,
Five, six, seven,
Eight, nine, ten,
Hundred, thousand, ten thousand.

The *Yamato-damashi*, the nationalist spirit which is responsible for much that is good and much that is evil in the nation's history, finds herein the most true account of the origin of the Koto of Japan, the Yamato Koto: and indeed its six long notches are there to this day to bear witness to it. The classical botanist, when he called that Kadzura tree "*K. japonica,*" emphasized another of the long-to-be-remembered incidents of that eventful day, for which service the *Yamato-damashi* is duly grateful.

The Encyclopædia, *Sansai Zuyé*—"All things in heaven and earth and the human brain set out and illustrated"—has christened Amé-no-Uzumé the "Japanese Apollo"; she is "the deity who invented music and gave it to humanity." To her is ascribed also the invention of the only other national instrument, the *Yamato Fuyé*, or Flute of Japan: otherwise called the "Bird from Heaven"—*Amé no Tori Fuyé*—which she made from bamboo gathered on the "Mountain of the Heavenly Fragrance," *Amé no Kaga Yama*, whence had also come those Kadzura vines which bound her hair: a trio of things celestial (*Amé no*), the mountain, the bird, and the Goddess. She added, so they say, the strains of this heavenly reed to the music of the bow-strings before the cave, while the Gods, creating then the principles of time, beat the measure upon the mother of all the Castanettes.

c

Probably owing to its divine origin, the Flutes have always been regarded as most sacred instruments. They are preserved with peculiar veneration, and for an extraordinary number of years : many of those now in use are said to be over a thousand years old. A list of the Temple Flutes was kept at Court, and, like most of the old instruments, they were known by special names : " The Snake-charmer," " Green Leaves," " The Fisherman," are among those which are still preserved.

Not until the twenty-second year of the Emperor Jimmyo—A.D. 835— does the Japanese Orpheus appear upon the scene ; not mythical at all, however, but very practical, in the person of a nobleman of the Court, who had for his Lute that most villainous of vile-sounding instruments, the Hichiriki. Yet, so they say, he played it so sweetly that one who had burglarious designs upon his property, hearing, went in unaccustomed innocence away. May-be the kindly mists of time have somewhat clouded the true perception of the burglar's state of mind. He must have fled in frightened horror ; for, of all the gruesome sounds ever invented by man, the Hichiriki gives forth the most unearthly.

Then there is the story of the pirate who was vanquished, not by valorous deeds, but by the music of this wild reed coming from the decks of his intended prey, which caused him to bend his sails the other way in a vain attempt at flight. This, indeed, is a true story, for that same Hichiriki is still treasured in the land, wrapped in silken cloths in its fan-shaped box, whereon its name is written largely and legibly—*Kaizoku maru*—which means " The Pirate." Possibly, too, it was the soul of this very Hichiriki which was enrolled among the heavenly beings, and to whose honour a temple was built in Banshiu, the province of Harima, and called " *Hichiriki no Miya* "—" The

Temple of the Hichiriki." A strange fate has, however, intercepted worship at the shrine, for a great rock has fallen from the mountains in front of the doorway so that none can enter, and none have been able to remove it.

This terrible instrument, called sometimes the "sad-toned tube," in spite of those sweetly potent sounds which tradition ascribes to it, is the diapason of the old classical orchestra ; the cacophony of the music must be visited on its head, and not, as is too common, on that of the much-maligned Shō. This "octave mixture," as it may be called, is guilty, it is true, of strange chords ; but it is innocent of harsh sounds, and is, comparatively speaking, quite "bird-like," as the Japanese say. " Its music," says the poet, "is like the wind of spring murmuring in rocky caves ; the very nightingales come to listen and to sing."

The historian has been at pains to collect, in chemists' language, "traces" of music in the earliest of recorded times. He finds them in the weird hullaballoos of the funeral ceremonial of the hero Amewaka, which lasted eight days and nights, and at which "musical instruments were certainly used." He finds them too in the time of the great first Emperor of Japan, Jimmu Tenno — about six hundred and sixty years before Christ — who stands, as the Japanese consider, in spite of our own scholarly opinion to the contrary, in the border-land between mythology and history. The Imperial troops went to battle shouting, as other warriors have done in other countries and earlier ages ; but these songs of war are declared to have been in regular and metrical form.

History becomes more interesting, though the Western scholars will not yet let it be called reliable, at the beginning of the third century after Christ, concerning the reign of the Empress Jingo Kogo, who conquered Corea.

Before setting forth on her victorious journey, she worshipped, as in private and in public duty bound, at the ancestral shrines ; and all the authorities agree, to the intense gratification of the *Yamato-damashi*, that the instrument used to accompany the rites was in very deed the Yamato Koto. Takeno-uchi, the minister in attendance on the Empress, is said, by one more circumstantial than his fellows, to have played the instrument on the occasion.

The Yamato Koto and the Yamato Fuyé, the Koto and Flute of Japan, alone among early instruments are indigenous to Japan. China, with its instruments and its music, occupies almost the whole ground : and they were, from earliest times, borrowed and appropriated by the Japanese. Even the Empress Jingo, though she set forth to war with the sound of national music in her ears, included both musicians and musical instruments in the tribute to be paid by Corea after its conquest. These Corean musicians are said to have been the first to direct attention to the importance of selecting well-seasoned wood for the bodies of instruments, by the eagerness with which they rescued from the furnaces of the salt manufacturers on the coast the timbers of a shipwrecked vessel. Musical histories preserve with much particularity both the date—291 A.D.—and the name of the ship—"The Kareno." Afterwards, as communication between the Islands of Dai Nippon

Early Historical Records.

and the Kingdom on the mainland became more frequent, all the Chinese instruments and music which Corea possessed, together with expert musicians in great numbers, passed into and influenced Japan. More especially in the Soshun era—588 A.D.—young men were chosen for the musical profession, to learn their art at the feet of the Coreans, and to study specially the Kakko, the Drum of Southern China. Fifteen years later, in the Suiko era, three famous musicians, Mimashi,

Nakayoshi, and another whose name has perished with him, came from Kutara, an independent province of Corea, to teach the use of many instruments and much novel and delightful music. Two years later, a great number of students went to China to enquire for themselves at the seat of learning.[4]

At the beginning of the seventh century musical progress received a great impetus from the zeal of the Crown Prince Umayado. This illustrious Prince, called after his death *Shotoku-taishi*—" Prince of the saint-like virtue"—is the hero of all the chroniclers. He is described as the first architect, the first law-giver, the first to study the art of boat-building, the first true civilizer of Japan. He also invented the Ō-tsuzumi and the Ko-tsuzumi—the shoulder and the side Drums of Japan : the invention being, however, more properly described as an adaptation and modification of the old Tsuzumi of China. He is said also to have introduced Indian music into the country ; but neither at this time, nor a century later, when Indian dancers were brought over, did Indian music ever obtain much popularity in Japan.

The Kutara musicians speedily came under Prince Umayado's notice ; and his influence enabled them to found their school in the village of Sakurai, in the Yamato province.

In the reign of the Emperor Temmu—673 A.D.—both Corean and Chinese musicians are found playing in the Imperial Gardens, *Establishment of Chinese Music in Japan.* Chinese music having by that time long been firmly established in Court favour. And again, at the close of the century, its popularity was still in the ascendant, for Chinese musicians and dancers invariably performed at the banquets of the Empress Jitō.

In the first years of the next century the Emperor Mommu developed so great a taste for the foreign music, that to be learned in it was to be in the height of fashion ; and all who were, and all who would be, in the highest circles, devoted themselves eagerly to its study. To encourage an art which found such eager students the Emperor established a Musical Bureau, and constituted it as part of his household. Yet even here history is caught repeating herself : the Emperor Monmu doing no more for Chinese music than had been done ages before for the national music by his great predecessor and first of his line. For, says the Yamato historian, did not the greatest of Emperors, Jimmu Tenno himself, order the Lady Sarumé to attend to all the musical affairs of his Court ?

The new Musical Bureau was christened "*Gagaku Rio*": *Ga* meaning "tasteful," and therefore, in old days as in new, an equivalent to something but lately introduced from foreign parts. It grew yearly in importance. In 724 A.D., in the reign of the Emperor Shōmu, there were under its direct control thirty-nine principal Chinese musicians, eight from Corea proper, twenty-six from Kudara, four from Shinra, and sixty-two from Dora : Kutara, Shinra, and Dora being the three independent provinces of Corea. The instruments in use were the Hichiriki, the Flutes, the Shō, the Gongs, and the various Drums, large and small.

The chief work of the Bureau was the development of the study of the classical Chinese dance — the Bugaku — and of its more popular companion, the Sangaku, of which more hereafter. It may be noted here that the Bugaku in its original form is still performed on State occasions at the Palace in Tokyo. The dancers, many of them lineal descendants of the musicians of the Bureau, have a special establishment near the Kudan, where they practise and twice or three times in the year give full-dress entertainments, attended by the members and household of the Imperial family : and, more often still, private performances in the presence of the Empress.

For a full century the work of the Bureau is unrecorded. The year 935 A.D., however, marks a distinct step forward. The Emperor Jimmyo, himself a musician of no mean order, sent commissioners to China to make further enquiries. They returned with fresh stores of knowledge, and brought back a new instrument—the Biwa—which figures largely in the history of Japanese music proper. It was in this reign that the noble Hichiriki player unconsciously melted the heart of his burglarious visitor : so wide indeed was the spread of musical culture.

Such in briefest outline was the advent of Chinese music into Japan. Not all the *Yamato-damashi* in the world could resist it. So potent was it, that it seems almost to have crushed Japanese music, as in those days everything Chinese crushed everything Japanese, out of existence. What with travelling students, and commissioners, and Bureaux, and musicianly Emperors, the *Yamato-damashi* could scarce console itself with the memories of the good old days, four centuries before, when the Emperor Inkyo *Lingering Traces of the Old Music of Japan.* gave a great feast, and himself played the Koto—the true Yamato Koto. But the Priests remained faithful, and the national music was heard in the Temples at festivals, such as the *Daijo-é*—the grand harvest feast. And even the Emperor Mommu, though he devoted himself, perhaps too much, to advance the prosperity of his new Bureau, did not omit the annual custom—dating from the time of Onin, when the shipwrecked " Kareno " gave its timbers to the musicians—of summoning the Nara band to the ceremonial banquet at the Palace to play the old melodies with which, to the accompaniment of Koto and Flute—Yamato both—the tribute of fish and mushrooms had been brought to the Sovereign. Only in very troublous times, subsequently, was this venerable custom discontinued. The continued service of the two national instruments in the Temples earned for them the epithet *kami*—divine : and thenceforward they were known as the *Kami Koto* and *Kami Fuyé.* The songs which they accompanied were divided into two classes : the *Ō-uta,* or "grand singing," in which the chorus sang sitting, and the *Tachi-uta,* or "standing singing," during which they stood on the steps of the Temple. From these forms of primitive sacred music the Kagura—*Kami Asobi,* the divine playing—or true Temple music seems to have been developed, which has lasted through many centuries to the present day.

When the Court was at Nara, a special chamber—the *Seishido*—was set apart in the Palace for the performance of the Kagura ; and ever since the time of the Emperor Ichijō — 987 A.D.— this music has been the special accompaniment to the worship of the Sacred Treasures—the ceremony of the *Naishi-dokoro.* The performance took place in the garden of the Treasures, the musicians being ranged on either side, the hereditary conductor standing between them in the fullest of full dresses, and wearing his swords. The instruments used were the Yamato Koto, Yamato Fuyé, and Hichiriki. The more celebrated Temples, at Isé and Kyoto for example, had each their special version of the music.

Tradition bases the music of the Kagura on the very strains which Amaterasu in the earliest year found so soul-compelling. The performance is intended, in fact, to preserve the incidents of the cave in pious memory. The darkness of the world and the at length yielding dawn were typified by

今様北人雛

鳥居末全筆

the hours during which, in former times, it took place: from ten at night till four in the morning. A fire of sticks was kindled in front of the Treasures, as the fire had been kindled before the mouth of the cave. And the presence of the Gods themselves was something more than symbolized in the presence of the Emperor with all the nobles of his Court. The music itself is divided into many parts, each of them intended to signify some scene of the Drama of the Entreaty. Thus among the main divisions there are "The Illumination," and "The Assembly"; and the smaller sections are called *tori mono*—"the things to be brought,"—as "the bow," "the gohei," "the stick," "the sword," "the spear," "the bamboo leaves," and "the Kadzura bough."

The following are two verses of the song of the Kagura; in the first the allusion is to the Kadzura bough which Amé-no-Uzumé held in her hand when she danced before the cave.

Miyama ni wa
Arare fururaji
Toyama naru
Masaki no kazura
Irotsuki ni keri.

The autumn hail is surely falling on the Miyama mountain, for the pure Kadzura trees on Toyama are changing their colour.

Sasa no ha ni
Yuki furi-tsumoru
Fuyu no yo ni
Toyo no asobi o
Ssuruga tanoshiki.

It is pleasant to gather together on a wintry night when the snow is lying thick on the leaves of the young Bamboos.

Much of the old ceremonial has to-day passed away: the fire, indeed, is still kindled, but the time has been changed to more convenient hours, for the Princes of the Blood may not sleep during the celebration of the rites. Thus the tradition of the darkness has been forgotten; but the especial sanctity of the occasion is still maintained. It runs risk of being marred by the devices of the modern side of life: the conclusion of the performance in the Palace at Tokyo is telegraphed to Kyoto.

The modern offshoot of the Kagura is the short benedictory dance of the "scarlet ladies," with their jangle of bells and waving of fans, familiar to all visitors to the Nikko Temples. For a few *rin* the pilgrim gets his blessing, and passes on before it is half finished to look at the famous Nikko Cat; only the more pious of the country-folk linger till the last of the old lady's sedate steps have been accomplished. This dance, which does not occupy more than thirty seconds, is a very abbreviated form of the *Dai dai Kagura*, the Grand Kagura, which lasts upwards of two hours, and is only performed in return for some special offering to the Temple. This is more properly called *Ya otomé mai*—" the dance of the eight virgins "—and is not the true form of the old dance, whose name it commonly bears. It is performed by the full staff of eight dancers, who attend daily at the Temples to perform to those who need their shortened ministrations. A much longer benedictory measure is gone through by each of the dancers in turn. It is accompanied by a big Drum, two large Kakko, and Flutes. The Drums are different from those used in the Bugaku orchestra.[5]

Independently of this Temple music, short compositions, called *Ro-yei*, in which Chinese poetry was used, made their appearance at a very early period. Being more easily remembered than the classical music, they acquired some popularity, especially among the educated classes. It is very uncertain what their form was ; but some definite form they must have had, the chronicler mentioning a collection of ninety *ro-yei*, made " and published " about the year 1070.[6]

A rival of the *Ro-yei* is heard of in the Engi era, called the *Imayo*, or " present style of song." Traces of both have entirely vanished. This Engi

era, which extended from 901 to 922 A.D., was the Golden Age of old Japan. Poetry, music, dancing, the arts and the sciences, all flourished under the genial influence of the Court. For the delectation of the courtiers a band of female musicians and dancers was established, the dancers numbering one hundred and forty. By this band the taste of the musical world in its lighter phases was practically regulated ; it seems to have existed side by side with the already ancient Musical Bureau, which still had the Chinese classical dances under its especial protection. The band could make or mar a musician's fame ; success and popularity for a new composition were attained only by performance by these Court musicians. The chief Chinese orchestral instruments in use at this period were the following. For the Sōgaku, the Chinese orchestral music which included the accompaniments to the Bugaku and Sangaku dances, and a certain amount of music performed without dancing— the Hichiriki, the Flute, and the Shō, which supplied the harmonies ; the Taiko, or big Drum, in different sizes ; the Kakko, or small drum, and the Shōko, a small and very acute Gong. For the private performances in the Palace—the *Kagen-gaku* the Drums and Gong might be omitted : but stringed instruments were added, the Sō-no-koto the only form of the Chinese Koto which obtained a footing in Japan and the sonorous Biwa. In addition to these, for the modern forms of Kagura already noticed, the drums were changed to a big Drum without braces—Ō-daiko ; and a larger Kakko Ō-kakko, or Daibyōshi, the "grand time beater."

We must now revert to the introduction of the Biwa into Japan, about 935 A.D., as this instrument had a most important influence on the growth of modern Japanese music.

Introduction of the Biwa.

As it came from China it was a ponderous instrument, very rich and sonorous in its tones. The heavy *bachi* was grasped firmly in the hand, and was dragged slowly across the four strings, making harmonious open chords, emphasizing the measure of the stately dance. As it was used then, nine centuries ago, so it is used now: its original form preserved with the same religious care that has preserved the music which came with it, and the dances which it helped to accompany. But like all things else from China that came within the sphere of Japan's eclecticism, when it was put to Japanese purposes it underwent a transformation. While preserving its essential qualities of rich tone and open harmonies, and though still a massive instrument that must rest on the ground, its Chinese and somewhat uncouth solidity gave place to something lighter, more graceful, more refined. The shape of the *bachi* was altered so as to obtain freer and more rapid sweeps over the strings ; a fourth fret was added, and all the frets were raised. The finger pressing the strings behind the frets could produce five semitones in succession without touching the neck, and the strings passing over their broad flat edges gave forth strange bird-like trills, which, though they were unclassic in Chinese music, were utilized to the full in the music which was specially written for it by the singers of Satsuma, where it made its home, and whence it derived its name, the *Satsuma Biwa*. It was essentially a harmonic, and not a melodic, instrument : and its open chords made it admirably suited to the accompaniment of long heroic recitations and ancient songs of love and war, which are dear to the soul of Japan.[1] The chief among them is the famous *Heiké Monogatari*, a long, long story, taking some hours in the reciting, which tells of the conflict between the Heiké and the Genji clans, of the discomfiture of the Heiké, and the drowning of the

infant Emperor Antoku.   This story was first shaped, as they say, by the
blind musicians who fled with the infant Emperor's followers to Kagoshima,
in the province of Satsuma ; it was handed down as the Saga of the war,
and sung long afterwards to incite the descendants of the defeated clansmen
to admiration and revenge.   To this chanted story of that struggle, famous
and Eastern-world renowned—to the simple descriptive music, centuries old,
increasing in vigour as the battle waged, sinking into slow melancholy
cadences with the retreat of the vanquished, the people listen still in rapt
attention, in a solemn Japanese silence.   For is it not told still by one of
the few remaining lineal descendants of the pupils of the blind priest Jo-ichi,
who had it from the blind Ichi-botoké, himself a pupil of the man who, in
1445, gave it its present form ?   Of Ichi-botoké it is said that he sang with
so sweet a voice that it seemed scarcely human : the common people thought
in listening that he was indeed divine, that Buddha had reappeared.   The
accompaniment is of the simplest nature ; merely rhythmical beats on the
lower strings, with occasional taps on the wood, slowly drawn open chords,
or a series of rapid sweeps to and fro over all four strings, finishing with an
up-stroke on the fourth, with a pause to allow the trill of the string to be
heard.   The dexterity with which these rapid passages are executed
astonishes, but their simple appropriateness gives the whole composition,
without exaggeration, a charm which not all ancient music, even in the
West, can be said to possess.   It is rugged, as such ancient music must
be : almost devoid of melody.   One short lilting phrase, which has without
doubt descended to the modern music of the Samisen, alone dwells in
the memory ; and this, so far as my explorations extend, occurs in nearly
every composition.

So the family history of the Biwa is characteristic of all the imported instruments. The Chinese instrument was preserved, but there grew up by its side the Japanese instrument that sprang from it. From its use exclusively in the orchestra of the Bugaku dancers, the old Biwa came to be christened the Bugaku Biwa; but in Japan the Satsuma Biwa is the Biwa proper; it is often called the " Heiké-biwa."

The chroniclers note the formation of a special band of blind Biwa players, drawn, it seems, entirely from Kagoshima, for the service of the Court. There were thus three distinct branches of music competing for popular favour—three bands of musicians specially under the Imperial patronage: the Gagaku Rio, the Bureau with its Chinese and Corean musicians, which preserved the imported music in all its classical rigidity; the Court band of female dancers and musicians, to whose hands the development of the national dances was confided: and the band of Biwa players.'

Much of the modern song music for the Samisen owes its origin to
Influence of the Biwa on the National Music. the Biwa music; and there is no doubt that, in its descriptive methods it had also an important influence on the national dance music. Inspiration for the dances was sought in the common incidents of daily life. The characteristic features of the incident were reduced into rhythmic form; and this was surrounded with the stereotyped common forms of dance movement and gesture, just as one would make a phrase the subject of a musical composition, weaving with it the commoner forms of musical expression.

Thus the national Saiba-gaku (*Seibara* in the vulgar tongue), invented in the Engi era 901 A.D. and which remained famous and popular for many years after, was based on the peasants' songs as they trudged over the mountains with the pack-horses, bringing tribute to the Emperor. This dance, with fifty-three varieties of songs, is said to have been " established as music by Imperial order," and was for a long time performed annually at the Palace. It is occasionally, though rarely, heard now.

The following are two verses of the song of the Saiba-gaku. There is a curious construction in the poetry, which involves the repetition in the third line of the subject of the second.

Idé waga koma wa	Oh, my pony,
Hayaku yuki-kosé Matsuchi yama,	Hasten past the Matsuchi mountain;
Awaré Matsuchi yama waré.	Oh, fair Matsuchi mountain !
Ao-yagi wo	Weeping willow-tree.
Kata-ito ni yorité oké ya	Twist thy single silken strands into a perch
Uguisu ni oké ya.	Whereon the nightingale may perch.

The same idea seems in later times to have led to the reduction into regular forms of the humming accompaniments to daily occupations, and to which characteristic names were given.[3] Thus there is *Cha-tsumi uta*, the " Tea-pickers' Song"; *Mari uti*, the " Song of the girls playing at ball"; *Ta-uyé uta*, the " Rice-planting Song ;" *Usu-hiki uta*, the " Mortar Song," sung by two girls pounding rice or tea in a mortar, to the rhythmical beat of the pestle ; and *Bon-odori uta*, the moonlight dance of fisher peasants in July, when the boys and girls danced through the village shouting, " Come and join the dance," and, perpetually adding to their numbers, finished their frolic on the sea-shore. So again the same idea has led to the invention of many of the charming *geisha* dances of the present day : the most graceful among them all, the " Bleachers' dance," is known probably to all who have travelled in Japan ; the dexterous waving of the long strips of white cotton, the characteristic poses of the three girls, dwell in the memory as the most delightful of recollections among a whole world of delights.

So, going back again into the regions of antiquity, we find almost an epoch of musical history marked by the introduction of such a song and dance—the Dengaku—the song of the rice-planters, which was "ordered to be established as music." To the accompaniment of Flutes and the Drums Taiko and Ō-tsuzumi, the Dengaku lived in Court favour until the close of the twelfth century, when, in the time of Yoritomo, the Sarugaku, the purest form of the Nō dance of the present day, was established. The rice-planters' dance fled to the provinces, reappearing intermittently in more modern times. It is said to have been performed at Mito two hundred years ago, by, it is almost needless to add, descendants of the original dancers; and yet again, only a hundred years ago, in Kishiu; and still later for a period at Nikko, on the occasion of the festival of the Shogun Iyeyasu. But, with Japanese particularity, the historian adds that at Nikko they did not perform the true Dengaku: for the Kakko, the small stand-drum, was added to the orchestra.

It will be convenient in this place to trace the distinction between
The Chinese and
Japanese Dances.
Chinese and Japanese dancing, both being current to-day. The dances and music which came from China were of two kinds: the severe classical Bugaku, to which reference has been made; and the Sangaku—literally "leisure dance," or "leisure amusement." This was of a light character, and more appealing to the popular taste: the severe Chinese mind attributing its invention, in a general sort of way, to the "foreign barbarian." The music was used chiefly to accompany comic acting and acrobatic performances. In the Musical Bureau, both Bugaku and Sangaku were studied, but they were performed by different bodies of musicians.

On the other hand, the Dengaku was purely Japanese in its origin ; and so also was its rival the Sarugaku. In the intervals of the Sarugaku light comedy pieces were performed, called Kiōgen ; and these seem gradually to have supplanted the Chinese Sangaku, which after a time went out of vogue. The word Sarugaku, however, dropped the " ru," and was very easily confused with Sangaku ; and, although the two dances had no connection, the old Chinese word came to be applied to the newer Japanese dance, which thenceforward was called " Sarugaku " or " Sangaku " indiscriminately.

In much later years the Bugaku remained as the amusement of the Court, the Sarugaku of the Shogun and Daimyo, the most wealthy of the nobles having their own theatre and dancers, together with a costly wardrobe of sumptuous brocade and embroidered dresses. In the present day, the Sarugaku and Kiogen dancers, like the Bugaku dancers, have their home in Tokyo ; their theatre adjoins the " Maple Club "—*Kōyō-kwan*—in Shiba Park, where they give frequent performances. Six or eight pieces of each class are given, the performance beginning at ten in the morning and lasting till six in the evening.

Both Bugaku and Sarugaku are popularly called Nō dancing ; the word *nō* signifying ability in any art. Strictly speaking, however, the Nō dance is a still later development of Sarugaku, standing midway between the old and the modern Japanese dances. Just as the old Japanese dance infused a little life and action into the old Chinese methods, so the Nō infused still more vigour into the Sarugaku, and incorporated the ideas and spirit of the times.

The Sarugaku appears to have achieved popularity rapidly, though invention was slow. By the middle of the thirteenth century no more than

E

sixteen standard pieces had been invented and approved. The orchestra consisted only of the Yoko Fuyé the Flute, and three Drums—the Utadaiko, Ō-tsuzumi, and Ko-tsuzumi. There was also a voice part, the song itself being called *utaï*. Later, these *utaï* were composed separately, and were recited without music. A collection of two hundred was published about the year 1500, most of them composed by Se-ami, son of Uizaki Iro, buffoon to the Shogun Ashikaga. The son of Se-ami, Oto-ami, founded the now-existing house of Kanzi, which is in fact the true and original family of Nō dancers. Four other ancient houses are still flourishing, but they date only from the later years of the sixteenth century. The Kiogen, or light interludes, were invariably unaccompanied. The later varieties of the Nō seem to have had no larger orchestra than the classical models, that is, Flute and Drums. In one instance only, the boys' Fan-dance — *Ennen* — brass Cymbals were added. In the modern Nō dance, however, the orchestra is composed of three Samisens in unison, with the Ō-tsuzumi and Ko-tsuzumi, and one reciter.

The accompanying illustration shows the classical Nō orchestra in full-dress. The black lacquer cap—"*yeĕshi*"—is never removed even before persons of the highest rank.

The separate *utaï* which have been referred to were composed chiefly by the priests: the words were based upon the Buddhist books, and the performance much resembled the Temple incantations. They were, moreover, invariably written with a double meaning, and were used as an indirect means of conveying instruction to the people, a notion derived from the old Chinese priesthood. The performance of the Sarugaku indeed at one time passed almost entirely into the hands of the priests: and many of the

ORCHESTRA OF THE CLASSICAL NŌ DANCE.

Temples used it as a substitute for the Kagura, maintaining special performers for the purpose. In the same way the words of the comic Kiogen were invariably written with double meanings, but with a view to imparting a different kind of information to a different class of people. The Daimyo living in their palaces, secluded from the commoner branch of humanity which served them, and surrounded by a band of attendants through whom information filtered but slowly, and purged of all unpleasantness, knew but little of the smaller matters which were going on outside. Special information as to any hardship which the people were suffering, or wrongs which needed redress, was conveyed to the Prince's ear by a dexterous use of the second meanings. The subtle play of meaning is a thing which delights the Japanese mind, and one with which they are very familiar; and it is said that these comedies rarely failed in giving the necessary information to the lord for whose amusement they were provided.

It is to be noted that women took part in the dancing of the Nō. They are now indeed banished from the Japanese stage; but they hold an important position in its history.

Okumi of Izumo, a young female Temple dancer, is the reputed inventor of the Kabuki, the Buddhist incantation and dance, *The Early Japanese Theatre.* accompanied by Flute and Drums. Leaving the Temple she performed the dance on a small stage in Kyoto; gradually enlarging the scope of the incantation, as well as its character, she developed it into a sort of play, in the performance of which she took the men's parts, while her husband, Sanjiro, took the women's. The new plays grew in popularity, until the Government, in 1643, suspended them on account of their immoral tendencies. Okumi then substituted a dance by boys, who played both male

and female parts; but this, in 1657, was in its turn suspended by the
Government. Finally, the system of licensing theatrical performances was
adopted, the licence being confined to pieces in which all the characters
were taken by men, and this system remains to the present day, so far as
the theatre proper is concerned.   Popular taste remained satisfied with the
early orchestra down to the middle of the seventeenth century: about 1640
the Samisen was first used in the Theatre to accompany the incidental songs.
It was introduced by the founder of the now-existing house of Kineya.

The Orchestra of the Modern Theatre is composed of two Samisens,
one Flute, and three Drums—the Uta-daiko, Ō-tsuzumi, and Ko-tsuzumi; the
Samisens having been added to the orchestra of the Nō.   There are also
two reciters.   It is called the "*Hayashi-kata*," the "accompaniment party."
The illustrations show this orchestra both in undress and in full dress.   The
latter is called "*Dega tari*'—"the orchestra which appears"; the full dress
being worn on certain special occasions, when it appears on the stage in
short one-act pieces, and occasionally in scenes in longer plays, by way of
accompaniment to soliloquies or solo dances.   In ordinary cases, however,
the orchestra is behind the scenes, and the full dress is not worn.

The Female Orchestra, "*Shita kata*," for accompanying dancing, is
composed of the same instruments, but without reciters.   From the illustration it will be seen that the Ō-tsuzumi and the Ko-tsuzumi are played by
the same performer, as the music does not require these two drums at the
same time.

Early Japanese Songs.   The gradual growth of music apart from dancing has been
chronicled with a refinement of precision and discrimination

THE ORCHESTRA OF THE MODERN THEATRE—IN UNDRESS

THE ORCHESTRA OF THE MODERN THEATRE—IN FULL DRESS

1

peculiarly Japanese. Apart from the number of Japanese names which it would involve, it would be impossible to attempt even a partial description of the classifications, which are based on lines quite unfamiliar to us. Solemnity and lightness, loudness and softness, the greater or sparing use of large intervals : these are some of the characteristics which differentiate one class from another. The composer who used a different characteristic from his predecessor in popular favour is invariably said to have invented a "new kind of music." Thus we find that the "new music" of the Kwanyei and Shōhō eras, invented by Satsuma Jōun of Izumi, was of a "very sober, decent kind," his themes being the valour and deeds of the ancient heroes. Satsuma Jōun had a pupil Toraya Genjitsu, who, having settled in Yedo, made a reputation by inventing music of a less solemn kind. His pupil was Inouye Harima, a learned man and fertile composer. His most celebrated pupil was Takemoto Chikugo, who is handed down to fame as the inventor of "an entirely new class of music made by mixing all the others up together." He also is celebrated as the inventor of the "*Gidayū-bushi*," the music for the marionette stage which he had set up in Osaka.

The marionettes achieved a great popularity, Takemoto being assisted by Chikamatsu Monzayemon—the "Shakespeare of Japan"—who supplied the books of the words. But the music was somewhat loud and vulgar. Miyako Itchū of Kyoto therefore invented "softer songs"—"*Itchū-bushi*" ; but these, as well as the "*Bungo-bushi*," so called after their composer, Miyakoji Bungo, degenerated into indecency, and were suppressed by the Government. They were afterwards started afresh in Yedo by Miyako Bunyemon ; but he found their music too soft and languorous for popular taste. He therefore made

a new departure with the "*Tokiwazu*"; and presently Tomimoto Buzen, a
performer of the *Tokiwazu*, invented the songs named after him, the "*Tomimoto-bushi*"; and Kiyomoto Enjusai, in the Kwansei era, invented his songs,
the "*Kiyomoto-bushi*"; and Uji Kadayū of Kyoto invented his, the "*Kadayū-
bushi*"; and Fujimatsu, a descendant of Miyakoji, invented his, the "*Fujimatsu-
bushi*"; and so the classification goes on, *ad infinitum*.   The "*Shinnai*"
invented by Tsuruga, a pupil of Fujimatsu, were songs of a low order and
an indecent character : the music is described as "very sweet and bird-like."
These, however, like their predecessors, the "softer songs" of Itchū, were
condemned by a troublesome Government.   All these, however, really
belong to one class, the "Joruri," so called after the first of the kind,
the "*Joruri Monogatari*."   This had sprung in direct succession from
the famous "*Heiké Monogatari*," to which reference has already been
made, the Samisen being substituted, in accompanying, for the Biwa.   Like
the Heiké song, the Joruri was a recitative accompanied by solemn open
chords and descriptive music ; it dealt, however, with a softer theme than
war and defeat—the prayer of aged parents to the Gods for a child : the
answer to the prayer and birth of a daughter : the naming of the child
Joruri Himé, "the maid from Paradise": the youth and maidenhood of the
lovely girl : and the love for her of Yoshitsuné.

The softer ideas of the *Joruri Monogatari* thus led to the development
of the numerous subordinate classes already mentioned.   They led, too, to
the creation of another distinct class of songs.   In the Keicho era, about
1620, Sawazumi, a very skilful Biwa player, departed from the strict tradition
of his profession, and sought fresh fields of fame in Samisen playing and
the study of the *utaï* of the Sarugaku dance.   A combination of the Joruri

THE DANCE ORCHESTRA

recitation and these *utaï* occurred to him, and his novel compositions led to the invention of the *Ha-uta* and *Ko-uta*, short poems or proverbial sayings which became very popular during the Ashikaga dynasty: from these again developed the *Naga-uta*, or "long songs," which included many classes : they were first composed by Tobaya Tanyemon of Tokyo, in the Enkyo era, about 1744. Two of the composer's many pupils founded two still existing families of musicians. In the Bunroku era, 1592 A.D., many varieties of *Ko-uta*, especially the "*Ryutatsu-bushi*," prevailed : they were accompanied by the Samisen and Shakuhachi. The Samisen was then fast becoming the popular instrument which it is at the present day.

In the following list are given all the varieties of the songs which sprang from the *Joruri Monogatari*, as indicated above : these songs are generically termed "*Joruri-bushi*." The Encyclopædia gives them as springing immediately from the "*Gidayū-bushi*," and the greater number of them as having been, like those, specially composed for the performances of the marionettes. Out of the somewhat long list, although many are still heard occasionally, the only survivors in popular favour at the present time are the two forms of "*Gidayū-bushi*," the "*Shinnai*," which seem to have braved the storm of Government indignation, and the "*Tokiwazu*."

I have added, further, a list of the songs which come under the head of "*Ha-uta*" and "*Ko-uta*": and, also, for convenience of reference, a tabular scheme of songs, showing the chronological development of the songs, as well as a similar scheme for the Chinese and Japanese Dances.

A LIST OF VARIETIES OF "*JORURI-BUSHI*" WHICH SPRANG FROM THE "*JORURI MONOGATARI.*"

Jōun-bushi: the "New Music" composed by Satsuma Jōun of Izumi in the Kwanyei and Shōhō eras.

Genjitsu-bushi: the songs invented by Toraya Genjitsu of Yedo, pupil of Satsuma Jōun.

Harima-bushi: the songs invented by Inouye Harima, a pupil of Toraya Genjitsu.

Kadayū-bushi, c. 1670: the songs invented by Uji Kadayū of Kyoto.

Gidayū-bushi, 1675: the music for the marionette stage invented by Inouye Harima's pupil, Takemoto Chikugo at Osaka, whose professional name was Gidayū.

The *Harima-bushi* seem to have been characterised by a long droning intonation: while the *Kadayū-bushi* were precisely the reverse, being sung with a short crisp accent. Takemoto Chikugo combined both these qualities in his songs. Between 1712 and 1731, two varieties were introduced by two of Gidayū's pupils: the first, pathetic songs written by Takemoto Harima, known to the profession as Gidayū the Second; the other, songs in a lighter vein, composed by Toyotaki Wakatayu. Both are still extant.

Bunya-bushi, 1681: marionette music invented by Okamoto Bunya, a pupil of Yamamoto Tosanojo, and a singer of *Gidayū-bushi.* His songs went out of fashion in 1704.

Itchu-bushi, 1688: marionette music composed by a priest Miyako Itchu, also a pupil of Yamamoto Tosanojo, who was a famous singer of the "*Joruri Monogatari.*"

Bungo-bushi, 1716: derived from the *Itchu-bushi* by Miyakoji Bungo, a pupil of Itchu.

Tokiwazu, 1736: the ultimate development of the *Bungo-bushi,* invented for the marionette stage by Miyako Bunyemon of Yedo.

Katō-bushi, 1716: invented by Katō Tōjurō, the son of a fishmonger, whose fondness for *saké* drove him to bankruptcy. His songs are still heard occasionally.

Fujimatsu-bushi, 1744: derived from the *Bungo-bushi* by Fujimatsu Satsuma, a pupil of Bungo.

Tomimoto-bushi, 1748: derived from the *Tokiwazu* by Tomimoto Buzen, a pupil of Bunyemon. His songs are still extant.

Shinnai-bushi, 1751: indecent songs invented by Tsuruga Shinnai, a pupil of Fujimatsu, which seem to have been revived in a purer form after their condemnation by the Government.

Sonohachi-bushi, 1751: derived from the *Bungo-bushi* by Miyakoji Sonohachi, and still occasionally heard.

Kiyomoto-bushi, 1804: derived from the *Tomimoto-bushi* by Kiyomoto Enjusai.

A LIST OF VARIETIES OF "*HA-UTA*" AND "*KO-UTA.*"

Ryūtatsu-bushi, 1592: short songs for the Samisen, composed by a priest named Ryūtatsu, who afterwards became a merchant-chemist: afterwards sung with Samisen and Shakuhachi.

Rosai-bushi: songs for Samisen and Koto, composed of 31 characters, developed out of the preceding by a priest named Rosai: their date is uncertain, but they were still in vogue at the beginning of the eighteenth century.

Naga-uta-bushi: "long songs": so called because they were lengthened developments of the songs included in the Ryūtatsu and Rosai class. They were composed by Ukon Genzaëmon, and are described as "very soft."

Shiba-kaki-bushi, 1655: songs and comic dances of a low character, in which the gestures were made chiefly with the hands. They went out of fashion in 1683.

Okazaki-bushi, 1661: songs and step-dances of a low character, still extant.

Magaki-bushi, 1658 to 1718: songs of the "Shim-machi," or Ōsaka Yoshiwara.

Doté-bushi, 1661: songs sung outside the Yoshiwara at Yedo.

Kaga-bushi, 1658 to 1674: songs of the Kaga province based on the Ryūtatsu and Rosai.

Dōnen-bushi, 1684: songs to accompany dances.

Nazé-bushi, or *Tsugi-bushi,* 1684: small songs popular in Kyoto: "up and down" songs.

Kokon-bushi, 1688: songs composed by the actor Kokon Shinzaëmon.

Komuro-bushi, c. 1688: according to some, songs sung before the Daimyo during their progresses to Yedo: according to others, songs sung by the *betto* as their masters were going to the Yoshiwara.

Ōsaka ko-uta: songs of Ōsaka, accompanied by Samisen and Koto.

Daijin-mai-no-kouta, 1716: the "rich man" song and dance.

Sazanza: songs in vogue in 1596.

Hosori: songs in vogue in 1661.

Kamigata-uta: songs of the "Kamigata," *i.e.* Ōsaka and Kyoto.

Torioï uta: the wandering minstrels' songs.

Bon-odori uta: moonlight dance of peasants on the sea-shore in July.

Yotsudake uta: a song accompanied by the Yotsudake, or "four bamboos."

Cha-tsumi uta: the tea-picking song.

Mari uta: the girl's ball song.

Sumiyoshi-odori uta: the chant of the priest of the Temple of Sumiyoshi when accompanied by his umbrella-bearer.

Ta-uye uta: the rice-planting song.

Usu-hiki uta: the pestle and mortar song, sung by two girls pounding tea or rice.

Isé-ondo uta, the Isé song: the guests are seated in the room, the dancers and the orchestra— Koto, Samisen, and Kokyu—being on gallery running round the room, which is gradually raised during the performance.

Kiyari: the name given to the workmen's shouting at the *matsuri,* and at the feast held when the foundations of a new building have been laid.

The form of the song is supposed to have originated 400 years ago: the old bell of the Kenjūgi Temple at Kyoto had fallen into the river, and the coolies when they were dragging it out were told each to scream his own name in chorus.

According to another story, Nobunaga the Shogun ordered the coolies who were dragging the stones for the foundations of his castle to scream together, but anything they liked.

A SCHEME OF DANCES AND MUSIC.

CHINESE.

Ga-gaku

- Bugaku (*public dancing*)
- Kagen-gaku (*private dancing*)
- Sangaku (*comedy*)
- Sōgaku (*orchestral music with or without dancing*)

JAPANESE.

Kagura—Kami-asobi
- Ya-otome-mai (dai-dai-kagura)
- Shintō Temple benedictory dance

Azuma-asobi

Saiba-gaku (Saibara) —*tribute song*—

Dengaku —*rice planters' song*—
- Kabuki
- Modern Theatre
- Kyōgen

Sarugaku (Sangaku)
- Enen (*boys' fan dance*)
- Modern "Nō" dance

A SCHEME OF JAPANESE SONGS.

Ro-yei

Imayo (*present style of song*)

Uiai of Gagaku (*Samizen*) [*Combined by Sawazumi in the Kéichō era.*]

- Ha-uta = Ko-uta
- Ryutatsu-bushi = Rosai-bushi
- Naga-uta
- many others
- many others

Heiké Monogatari (*Biwa*)
- Joruri Monogatari (*Samizen*)
- Satsuma Jōun's "New Music"
- Toraya Genjitsu's Songs
- Inouye Harima's Songs = Uji Kadayu's Songs
  - Gidayū-bushi
    - Gidayu the Second's "Gidayu-bushi"
    - Toyotaki's "Gidayu-bushi"
  - Sonohachi-bushi
    - Bungo-bushi
      - Shinnai bushi
      - Fujimatsu-bushi
        - Tomimoto-bushi
          - Kiyomoto-bushi
    - Itchu-bushi
    - Bunya-bushi
  - Tokiwazu

THE SHAKUHACHI PLAYER.

The Shakuhachi, introduced into Japan from China by Prince Tsuneyoshi as far back as the year 1335, seems to have *Introduction of the Shakuhachi.* been treated from the first as a solo instrument, with the one exception already noted, that it was sometimes used in accompaniments with the Samisen; it figures nowhere in the orchestra. Its use in the country, and the great admiration which the beauty of its tone evokes among the Japanese, are not the least curious of the problems which the study of the music of the country presents. How the Shakuhachi can have given pleasure to people who delighted in the gruesome dronings and wailings of the Hichiriki: how the Hichiriki can have been tolerated by ears which had once listened to the mellow notes of the Shakuhachi, are questions of musical pathology which it is not given to us to understand. The two instruments are, indeed, at the opposite poles of sound. Nor is it possible to say that the Shakuhachi is the only beautiful sounding instrument in use: the pipes of the Shō give delicate notes of no little beauty, if they are used alone; but, unfortunately, they never are used alone, such is the contrariety of this music. The greater Drums, too, are full and rich-toned; and the tones of the Temple Gongs float through the air in the gentlest of musical murmurings.

The tones of the Shakuhachi have woven pleasant fancies round its early history. So sweet were they that they travelled from the cave of its hermit inventor, through the still midnight ether, straight to the Emperor's Palace. They mingled with his dreams, telling as in a song where the magician dwelt whose slaves they were. On the morrow the Emperor sent to find him, and lo! the dream was true.

By way of more sober and veracious history, I have yet in my mind the memory of a dark night, when we sat on the verandah of a tea-house

in the mountain village of Chiuzenji ; the lake was lit by a thousand candles
stuck on to slight rafts of wood, votive offerings drifting slowly over the
water into eternity, and bearing on their way the prayers of the pilgrims
who had launched them to the shrine on the opposite shore. And there
suddenly came across the waters the soft clear tones of this simple pipe,
which filled me in those earliest of days in Japan with wonder that any
sound so sweet should come out of this very Galilee, so they say, among
the unmusical nations.

Thus far, as clearly as it can be traced, but with, I fear, too much
infusion of uninteresting detail, and reference to names unknown and things
not very intelligible without example and illustration, the history of old
Japanese music : old as to its origin, but still practised, still performed, and
still listened to with intelligent interest by large audiences of all classes. I
must turn now to the modern music of the country.

The Modern Music
of Japan.
The modern music is practically synonymous with Koto
music. Generically it is called *Koto-uta*—songs for the Koto ;
in it we find a more clear expression of the Japanese character. Freed
from the weight of Chinese influence : freed from the inharmonic chords
of the Shō, the imperfect lipping of the Flutes, and the coarse discord-
ance of the Hichiriki, and dependent entirely on stringed instruments, it
acquired a more definite intonation than the classical music, and developed
distinct melodies, recognisable even to Western ears, which are characterised
by the grace and minute quaintness of the national idea. Exceptions
to this are indeed numerous : many even among the more elementary
compositions, fail altogether of significance to us ; but this seems to be

due, not to fault on either side, but to those fundamental differences of idea which must inevitably exist between two entirely distinct races — differences of idea which find expression not in their music alone, not in their arts alone, but in every phase of their thought and existence.[16] Of this unintelligible music I may give one example in the following tune called "*Aké-no-kané*"—the "Bells at Dawn."

AKÉ-NO-KANÉ—(The Bells at Dawn).

I do not imagine that this little piece will find many admirers; it is not indeed a fair example of the better qualities of the music, some at least of which will be found in the four examples given later—"*Hitotsu-toya*," "*Saita-Sakurai*," "*Matsuzu-kishi*," and "*Kasuga-mōdé*"; and with regard to these, and

the many others which resemble them, among the popular songs, the point
which seems to me of interest is that there is so much in them which not
only is easily retained by Western memory, but which distinctly satisfies the
canons of Western taste. Many are the little haunting melodies one hears
tinkled in the street; many a one even commends itself to the whistling
Briton. Is not this indeed, as one has somewhere said, one of the tests
of the true inwardness of music? This incomprehensible music must,
however, not be confused with the more rigid and complicated forms
of Koto composition, classical music as it may be aptly termed. This is
no more to be called incomprehensible than the rigid and classical compositions of the West. It is distinctly of a high quality; it is based on an
elaborate system of form to be presently examined; but it requires close
attention, some musical training, and at least intelligent understanding
to appreciate it. Unfortunately, the circumstances under which we are
accustomed to listen to this music are not too favourable to very close
attention: it comes but as the interlude to a Japanese feast: occasionally
something specially bright and sparkling divides attention with the other
graces of the feast, and secures a meed of applause; but this is all, the
same piece is rarely heard a second time, and there is no intelligible
score available at which the foreigner can refresh his memory. So the
thing passes; it has brightened a few moments of the evening, and has
fulfilled the end for which it was created. But the science of its creation,
the dexterous skill of its execution, pass unheeded, or, if noticed hastily,
are as speedily forgotten. To the Western musician there is another
serious impediment to the spontaneous appreciation of this Koto music in
the absence of strongly marked and regular accent. It flows on the even

tenour of its way, full of interpolated "graces," full of quaint "accidentals," full
of curious rhythm, but the accent falls a little promiscuously, and our notion
of regular time is apt to be not a little shocked. And yet, strange to say,
it appears perhaps to be the strangest thing of all when one discovers it,
the music is built upon a regular scheme of "two-four" time, and the
necessity of keeping time is dinned into the pupils as remorselessly in
the Japanese as in the Western schools.

There are then classical compositions, as well as popular songs, in
modern Koto music. The songs are not fettered by formal   *Koto Music.*
rules, but there is a strong tendency to run to eight-bar phrases. The
classical compositions are subject to the most rigid rules. They are divided
into two classes : *dan* and *kumi.* The *d.n*—"steps"—are progressive studies
without singing, built on leading themes, increasing gradually in complexity.
The number of the steps varies from five to nine : thus there are pieces
named "*Go-dan,*" "*Roku-dan,*" "*Shichi-dan,*" "*Hachi-dan,*" "*Ku-dan*"— the
five, six, seven, eight, and nine "steps." Each *dan* is composed of fifty-four
bars, two crotchets to the bar. The "*Kumi*" are songs with elaborate
accompaniments, the parts corresponding with the verses of the poem ;
they also are built on leading themes, giving the effect of "airs with
variations." There are four verses at least, but generally a greater number.
Each verse is divided into eight sections, and each section into eight bars ;
the length of the parts, sixty-four bars, is thus greater than the length
of the *dan.* The bars are called *hyoshi,* like the bars of the Chinese
music, and, as I have said, though our ears do not catch it at once,
except for an occasional *rubato* passage, time is kept rigidly throughout
the performance. Directly, indeed, the original intimate connection between

the two classes of music is realised, it becomes evident that, however the
Japanese offspring may have wandered from the austere courses of its
Chinese parent, it could never shake itself free of the rigid time principle
which characterised its ancestor : a void formlessness, which we are so apt
to imagine the leading feature of Japanese music, was the very last thing
which was likely to come over it   I reserve, until I have described the
Drums, a fuller explanation of Chinese time.

The story of the rise of this modern Koto music takes us back through
some few centuries, to the time when angels and the higher powers were
wont to visit the islands of Japan.

Among the many things which stand out of the haze of time more or
less distinctly there is one interesting point very much in doubt : Which of
the many forms of the Chinese *Kin*, or *Koto*, came first to Japan, and the
manner of its coming.   The *Sō-no-koto* is the one now in use in the
Bugaku orchestra ; but a more cumbersome instrument, the *Hitsu-no-koto*,
is pointed to as the one which first came over the seas ; so delicate a matter
can be decided only by the researches of Japanese experts.   The current
story, given even by the sober-minded and accomplished Yamada Ryu in his
" Short Outlines of the Sō-no-koto and its Music," surrounds the coming
of the instrument with clouds, and mountain-tops, and lovely ladies.

There was in old time—more particularly, in the reign of the Emperor
Temmu, 673 A.D.—a Court lady, the Lady Ishikawa Iroko, who, for her
Origin of the Koto Music. health's sake, had left the Imperial service for awhile to
reside in Kiushiu.   Wandering one day on the slopes of
the mountain *Hikosan* to gather flowers, her footsteps strayed—or a soft
influence crept over her brain directing her footsteps—far into the recesses

of the mountain. Strains of a strange unknown music floated through the air, and led her at length to their source, a glade, wherein sat sedately a Chinese musician playing on the *Sò-no-koto.* Him she at first imagined to be a deity, so unconscious was he of her presence, so sweet the sounds he drew from the vibrating strings. But presently, when the music ceased, he saw that she had come whom he had desired should come. Then he spoke to her, seeing that she should convey his soft message to the people, telling her all the secrets and the mystery of his art. And as the days went by her fingers began to stray over the strings, at first aimlessly, impelled only by a feminine curiosity, but afterwards, with more purpose, as they yielded to the master's guidance. And the weeks and the months went by, until her skill was perfected, and her store of learning was complete. Then she descended from the mountain, bearing with her the Koto of the spell. But when she sought again the place wherein all this wonder had been wrought, lo! the grove and its musician had vanished, and a cloud only rested where it had stood. Truly therefore the Lady Ishikawa's first thought was the true one : the musician was a God indeed.

Her descendants taught this music to many people, even down to the reign of Gotoba the Emperor, at the end of the twelfth century, when it was known as "*Tsukushi-gaku*"—"Kiushiu music." So potent was it that it flourished still among all classes down to the reign of Gonara the Emperor, in 1527 A.D.

A difficulty occurs here which I have not been able to unravel. The date of the Lady Ishikawa's visit to the mountain Hikosan roughly coincides with the date given by other historians of the advent of Chinese music and the construction of the Musical Bureau. The story of the mountain may therefore be the legendary form of the history of the coming of this music. *Tsukushi-gaku*, however, is mentioned as something quite distinct from the Sōgaku and Bugaku music. Although all traces of it have been lost, it seems probable that a form of solo music for the Sō-no-Koto did exist in China, and that it came over to Japan at about the same time as the orchestral and dance music.

At this time the priests of Hizen were very accomplished musicians, and a short genealogy of priestly master and neophyte pupil brings us to the coming of the young priest Hosui, of the Zentōji Temple in Chikugo, to Yedo, in the reign of the Emperor Gomizu-no-o, in 1612.

Rise of Yatsuhashi.

He daily delighted audiences of rank and fashion, and the fame of his playing went abroad. It reached the ears of Yamazumi of Ōshū, a blind Biwa player of repute, who had already received the degree of "Kōtō." Eagerly the blind musician journeyed to the Eastern capital, and sat at Hosui's feet. The master became the young priest's pupil, and when the stores of his learning were exhausted, went to Hizen to learn of Hosui's master, Genjo. Thence returning to Yedo a perfect Tsukushi-gaku musician, he received the second degree of " Kengyō," and took the name Yatsuhashi; and he afterwards became the father of the modern Japanese Koto music, and the inventor of the Japanese Koto. The *Tsukushi-gaku* is described as being "very high class and solemn." Yatsuhashi, though a profound admirer, yet thought that it might give place occasionally to something lighter and more melodious, and that he might obtain a wider audience among the people. He gave his thought shape in the *kumi* which he gradually elaborated. For subjects he went to the famous romances of the period, the "*Isé Monogatari*" and the "*Genji Monogatari*," composing thirteen pieces : "one for each month and one over for leap-month," or "one for each string," according to the fancy. Within a very short time the grace of the new music appealed

successfully to the popular taste, and many *kumi* were composed by Yatsuhashi's pupils, who were then, by the rules of the profession, admitted to
the honour of founding a house of musicians.

In the meantime Hosui had become a layman, still teaching the Koto,
under the name of Kashiwaya. His former pupil, Yatsuhashi, then an old
man, became his master, and an intimate friendship sprang up between them,
Hosui adding many *kumi* to their joint repertoire. The master attained
to the highest proficiency, taking the third degree of "Sōroku." He then
elaborated a second series of compositions of a more severe kind, called at
the time "*Shin-kyoku*"—the "new pieces": the *dan*, to which reference has
already been made. Yatsuhashi's chief pupils through several generations
were Kitajima, Kurahashi, Mutsuhashi, Yasumura, Hisamura, Ishizaka,
Ikuta, and Yamada Ryu the most famous of them, who set down in his
book what he remembered of his master's teaching. They all received the
degree of Kengyō. Yatsuhashi's energy was not exhausted by his compositions; he turned his attention to making improvements in the Koto,
insisting chiefly on the selection of hard *kiri* wood (*Pawllonia Imperialis*)
for the sounding-board, and on its being thoroughly seasoned. His earliest
attempts he christened "*Akikiri Koto*"—the "Autumn-mist" Koto; and
"*Matsu-nami*"—the "Murmuring of the Pines" Koto. From these
afterwards developed the two forms of Koto now in use. The
"*Ikuta-koto*," so called from the name of its originator, Ikuta, a pupil of
the second generation from the master. Its sides and extremities are
covered with much inlay and lacquer ornament; but these are banished in
the "*Yamada-koto*" of Yamada Ryu. In this instrument the eye is gratified
only by the beautiful graining of the natural wood, a thing delighted in by

the purest Japanese taste; only occasionally a little severe gold ornament being permitted along the sides. The *Yamada-koto* is used by all professionals, as it has a clearer and more resonant tone than the more delicately built *Ikuta-koto*, which, though prevalent in the west of Japan, is used in the east almost entirely by lady amateurs. Like the Kin, the Koto is fantastically supposed to be a dragon, symbolical of all that is noble and precious, lying on the sea-shore, holding such sweet converse with the waves that the angels come to sit and listen by his side. And so the Oriental, his mind full and fond of quaint conceits, has given many curious names to the parts of the instrument in accordance with this mythical idea. The upper surface is the dragon's back; the under surface his belly. The upper part of the side is the sea-shore—*ō-iso*; the lower, *ko-iso*, the lesser shore. The oval of tortoise-shell at the right end of the upper surface is the sea—*umi*; the long bridge at the right end, the dragon's horn—*ryōkiku*; the long bridge at the left end, the horn of cloud, or the angel's seat—*temmyō*. The angular projection at the right end is the dragon's forked tongue—*ryō no shita*; the other end, *kashiwaba*, his tail. The cavity at the right end of the under surface is the "hidden moon"—*ingetsu*; and that at the left end, *marigata*, the "bowl-shaped place."

Note on Japanese Musical Degrees.

Special encouragement was offered to the blind to obtain proficiency in music, the house of Yoshida, of the Imperial Household, being empowered to confer on them ranks or degrees. The degrees were three : *Kōtō*, *Kengyō*, *Sōroku*, about ten years elapsing between the grant of each. The claim for a degree had to be supported by a recommendation from those in the same profession that the candidate was worthy of the honour : as a mark of great honour and esteem the suggestion would often be made in the first place by the profession. A subscription was generally made among the pupils for the necessary expenses and the fees, which were 100 yen, 200 yen, and 1000

THE WANDERING SAMISEN PLAYER

yen, for the three degrees respectively. Then came the pilgrimage to Yedo, the ceremonial presentation of the candidate, the payment of the money, three or four months of somewhat unnecessary delay, a refusal of the degree being unheard of, and, lastly, the information that the degree had been conferred, and that the money had been paid into the Imperial Treasury.

Blind "pin-prickers" shared with musicians in the three degrees just mentioned. The title of Shōjo, or Daijo, was also conferred on musicians who were not blind, Shintō priests, high-class fortune-tellers, and cake makers ; the rank was equivalent to Third Governor, and was conferred in connection with the name of a town, much in the same way as English titles are granted. A title would run thus : Inouye Harima no Shojo—the Shojo Inouye of Harima ; Takemoto Chikugo no Daijo—the Daijo Takemoto of Chikugo. A connection between the person ennobled and the place of his title was not essential. The whole business of conferring titles on professional men, except those who were recommended by the Shogun, was in the hands of the Yoshida family, a monopoly granted to them by the Emperor.

Monopolies formed the chief source of income of many of the Court nobles till the system was abolished at the time of the Restoration. Thus the teaching of the Sō-no-koto was entirely in the hands of the house of Yotsu Tsuji : the teaching of the Biwa in that of Fushimi, a prince of the blood : singing in that of Jimyōin. All certificates of proficiency, without which no teacher could exercise his profession, were signed by the head of the house holding the monopoly, and in many cases he himself would conduct the examinations. Other monopolies not connected with the subject in hand were the right to grant to football players the distinction of wearing lilac strings to their hats, vested in the house of Sakai : and to falconers lilac tassels for their falcons who had caught a crane. In the house of Takakura was vested the sole right of initiating into the mystery of Court dressing those who approached the Imperial presence.

Although the Koto is the national instrument, the Samisen is the instrument of the people. It is played by ladies of high and low *The Samisen.* degree, chiefly perhaps by those whose crest is the butterfly. A momentary pause in a peculiar thrumming, to which, with its accompaniment of weird nasal sounds, the ear soon gets accustomed in Japanese streets, tells you that the beggar is going her rounds and has received her dole—many doles make one penny ; a delicate tinkling in the air as you pass an open window tells you that the *geisha* is busy practising for her evening's entertainment— many practisings go to one five minutes' entertainment. The Samisen figures everywhere and on every occasion ; it accompanies dancing, acting, singing, begging, eating, drinking, everything almost except praying, and that is the smallest of exceptions. The sound is curiously complex, a mixture between thrumming and tinkling—in "Looking Glass" language, "thrinkling." The *bachi*, or plectrum, with its sharp pointed edges, strikes the strings with a downward and outward motion, but it meets the parchment face of the body first, making a drum sound before the string vibration is heard. When it forms part of the Chamber quartettes, in company with two Kotos and Kokyu, this drumming first attracts attention, the delicate twang of the strings seeming to come from some fifth and invisible instrument. It more often than not doubles the Kokyu part, but occasionally has more difficult passages written for it.

The Samisen is supposed to have come to Japan, about 1560, from Liu Chiu, where it was used more as a children's toy than as a serious musical instrument. To this dignity it was advanced by the Biwa players, who found it a more portable instrument than their own, and was first used for accompanying the "*Joruri-bu-hi.*" History has preserved to us the names of the earliest players—Nakanokōji and his pupil Torasawa, and later, in the Keichō era, 1596 A.D., Sawazumi, who was a master of the *Ko-uta* and other offshoots of the "*Joruri Monogatari.*" Sawazumi settled in Ōsaka; his two pupils, Kagaichi and Jōhidé, came ultimately to Yedo, where they created a great sensation with the new instrument—so great, indeed, that the chroniclers say that the second degree of Kengyō, with the names Yanagawa and Yamahashi, were "granted" to them. The remission of the customary fees due to the noble house of Yoshida, is, however, not recorded. Yamahashi *Kengyō* is regarded as the father of modern Samisen players: he gave the instrument the name *San sen*—"three strings," which was afterwards converted

瀬川菊之丞

國安画

into the three-character word *Sa-mi-cn*, or "three tasteful strings." Another but rather doubtful theory is that the instrument existed in Japan in the fifteenth century, at the time of the Ashikaga dynasty. It is probable, however, that it was in use in China during the twelfth century, and thence travelled to Liu Chiu. The belly was originally covered with snake's skin, and it was strung with two strings only, the third being added by one Ishimura.

The *Kokyu*, the Japanese Fiddle, the last of the trio of Chamber instruments, came from Hindustan to China; thence it *The Kokyu.* travelled through Liu Chiu to Japan. It is described in the Encyclopædia as having been originally used by the southern barbarians to ward off the attacks of venomous reptiles on account of its mournful tone. Originally the bow was a miniature long archery bow, with one stout string; it is now made of a loose bundle of horsehair, two feet and a half long. Unlike the fiddle of the West, the Kokyu fulfils no function of any importance with regard to Japanese music: it is used only to emphasise the melody or important phrases in the Chamber quartettes, and but seldom, if ever, as a solo instrument. Indeed, the position in which the instrument is played, and the cumbersome bow with its heavy swaying tassel, prevent the execution of any elaborate passages. The player, as in the case of all other instruments, sits on the floor, with the Kokyu resting on its metal spike in front of the left knee. This spike serves as a pivot, enabling the instrument to be turned in order that the outer strings may be pulled clean. It is not often that one hears it well played; but in the hands of a professional the best instruments give forth a sweet and somewhat plaintive tone: all the notes on the doubled upper strings, though very delicate, are

exceedingly penetrating.   It is curious to note that the loose bundle of
horse-hair is as capable of making the sound float off the strings as the
tight-strung Western bow, and without the slightest suspicion of scratching.
It is, indeed, not the least remarkable example of the topsy-turviness of
things in general out in the East.

The capabilities of the instrument have, as I have said, never been
realised, and the reason is not far to seek.   In the first place, the teaching
knows nothing whatever of "positions;" the fingering is learnt entirely by
rote.   The pupil sits facing the teacher, and must copy the motions of her
hand and fingers.   With so crude a method of teaching—its difficulties
being recognised by a fee being charged which is double that for teaching
the Koto—the playing must inevitably become untrue; added to which, it
is often careless.   But, in the second place, the diatonic scale is not known
as such in Japanese music.   Any instrument which is capable of producing
the complete scale, of which only a selection of notes is used, is rather like
a hand with two fingers paralysed: they get in the way, and so do the
unfingered portions of the Kokyu strings.

The illustration shows the trio of Chamber instruments.   It is called in
Japanese "*Sankyo-ku awasé mono*"—"three instruments in harmony."   It is
generally heard at private parties, the instruments being often played by
amateur ladies of high rank.   At public entertainments a second Koto is
usually added.

One other instrument heard often enough — too often — I have not
Japanese Singing.   ventured to describe, nor shall I venture: the human voice.
Words would fail me were I to attempt to do justice to its peculiarities.   It
is mere horrid sound, disfigured by excruciating quarter-tones.   Nor have I

THE CHAMBER TRIO.

ever found a Japanese express any admiration for it. It is accepted and tolerated. But again there comes uppermost that perplexing query, how the curious mixture of sweet and unsweet sounds has been suffered to endure. Though there are many directions to the singer of Joruri—which I give in a note—to try and produce as sweet a sound as possible, not to sing coarsely, not to strain the voice, and not to make grotesque grimaces, to live soberly and temperately, for "bad conduct spoils both the character and the voice"; yet "smooth and sweet" singing never has any one heard in Japan. Therefore let the voice pass. Not so, however, the "quarter-tones." They are an integral part of the singing, and have to be produced correctly. Corresponding as they do with those produced on the Flute and Hichiriki, they are probably of Chinese origin. It has been supposed that they are real notes and form part of the scale; but, the books, so far as I have been able to ascertain, throwing no light on the matter, I can hardly accept this hypothesis. Indeed, I doubt if they are real notes at all. It is convenient to use the term "quarter-tone," but more accurately it is a slur up to the note through the tones contained in a quarter-tone, without any emphasis on the first tone. The quarter-tone sound is used, but so are all the intervening sounds, as in a "slide" on a violin, and therefore, although, like the "slide," the slur has to be produced correctly and with a certain art, yet it seems impossible to treat the quarter-tones as forming one of the definite series of notes on which the music is built.

Instructions for Samisen Players when performing Joruri.

[From the work on music by Miyakoji Bungo, the inventor of the *Bungo-bushi*.]

The performer should sit with his knees apart and in a straight line, the bookstand in front of him, and his head just level with the *kenzi*—the bookstand, and neither bent down nor with his chin too much in the air. When seated he should take his fan out of his *obi*, and place it horizontally across the book, moving it as he turns the pages one after the other. He must not do anything ugly, and therefore he should avoid too much motion; he should not force his voice in singing, and should refrain from making grotesque grimaces. Thus only will he be able to sing smoothly and sweetly. This is called *zashiki-sadamé*, or the method for determining the position of the body.

Next comes *chōshi-sadamé*, or the determination of the tone of the voice, which must vary in loudness or softness according to the size of the room. Therefore when the musician enters the room he should at once take a mental measurement of it, and determine on this matter immediately.

Next comes *hyōshi-uchi*, the rule of emphasis. The singer should mark the time with his fan (*hyōshi-ōgi*). He should avoid too much emphasis, but, thinking only of the circumstances of the song, let his mouth and heart work together and guide his hand.

Next comes *ishoku-sashi*, the consideration of the rank. The singer should accommodate his voice to the character of the person about whom he sings, whether it be a hero, for example, or a woman. Thus, if he sings of a priest he should be priest-like; or if of a woodcutter he should simulate his voice, and so forth.

Next comes *chōshi-omoi*, the consideration of the tuning. Now although our *Samisen* has only three strings, yet all the twelve sounds are there and to be played upon them. So the player ought to take deep consideration of all these twelve sounds.*

Next comes *onsei-tashimi*, the preparation of the voice in the chest, by opening the lungs. Now every phrase may be sung in two breaths; yet the singer must not avail himself of this rule and sing coarsely. He ought to try and produce as sweet a sound as possible, which can only be done by keeping the body in its proper position. So while singing he must not bow too much, but let the voice come from the chest. No human voice has a sound higher than *fushō*. Therefore straining to produce higher sounds such as *ōshō* must be avoided. This is called *uragoé*—the production of bad sounds.

Next comes *kwaigo-no-ben*, the consideration of opening and closing the mouth, so as to avoid a slovenly pronunciation of the words.

Opening the mouth is the male principle; it is equivalent to spring and summer: it is *ryo*. Shutting the mouth is the female principle; it is equivalent to autumn and winter: it is *ritsu*.

Finally comes *sekijō*, the consideration of the audience. If in the songs which are to be sung

---

* The twelve sounds are the twelve Chinese *ritsu* or semitones. This direction puzzles me somewhat; it may refer to one of two things, either to the pitch, as to which there is no special direction if this does not refer to it : or to the tuning of the instrument, whether *honchōshi*, *niagari*, or *sansagari*. It is quite possible, however, that it refers to both : that the singer is to be careful to select the right tuning for the music, lest it should miss any of its due effect by not getting the proper open notes ; and he must be careful, too, to pitch it so as not to strain his voice.

[handwritten annotations:]
C# – F# – C#

Further info see pg. 174.

C# – G# – C#   G# – C# – F#
tunings have no Relation to Key-
object Accuracy –

any fact is mentioned which would be unpleasant for any of the audience to hear, it should be omitted or altered ; and if any name is referred to which corresponds with the name of any person present, it should be changed, so that anything that might appear to be a personal reference may be avoided.

Finally, a singer should be temperate, drinking little, and of quiet sober conduct in his every-day life, for bad conduct spoils both the character and the voice.

A Table for the Production of Sounds—Kwaigo-no-ben.

The Chinese characters used for musical sounds were five in number :—

kyū   shō   kaku   chi or cho   u

but they are not simple sounds, and are more like syllables. Therefore the simpler *kana* sounds are used :—

a   i   u   e   o

These are called *go-sei*, or *go-in*—the "five voices,"—and these with different consonants pre-fixed are used for the formation of the voice according to the following table, the sounds of which are called the *gojū-in*—the "fifty voices" :—

a	ka	sa	ta	na	ha	ma	ya	ra	wa	open mouth
i	ki	shi	chi	ni	hi	mi	i	ri	i	closed ,,
u	ku	su	tsu	nu	fu	mu	yu	ru	u	,, ,,
e	ke	se	te	ne	he	me	ye	re	e	open ,,
o	ko	so	to	no	ho	mo	yo	ro	o	closed ,,
resonance in throat	in back teeth	in the teeth	on the tongue	on the tongue	on the lips	on the lips	in the throat	on the tongue	in the throat.	

These fifty sounds are also called the *sei-in*, or "clear voices" : then follow twenty more sounds called *daku-in*, the "thick voices" :—

ga	za	da	ba		pa
gi	ji	ji	bi	and finally five more, called	pi
gu	zu	dzu	bu	*jisei-in*—the "second clear voices"; or *handaku-in*—the	pu
ge	ze	de	be	"half-thick voices."	pe
go	zo	do	bo		po

I fear that, from what I have said on the subject of the singing of the
Japanese, there is but one conclusion : that the Japanese musician is not a
very musical person. I am not sure that this is capable of disproof. And
yet music is used to accompany almost every incident of daily life that is
in the least out of the common. I do not think that it could ever so move
this light-hearted people as music stirs the people of the West. There is
no evidence that Japanese music has ever occupied so high a position.
Scattered through all their " Myriad Leaves " there is but a verse now and
again which is due to its influence. And, withal, there is a strangely
romantic side to their nature which impels the utterance of tender nothings
to tender flowers, which, when their petals fly off upon the wind, are
nothings too ; which makes them think with a momentary sadness on the
mutability of human affairs and the uncertain flowing of the currents of
existence ; which makes them dwell the longer with appreciating glances and
soft words of delight on some small speck of beauty hardly coming within
the Western visual angle. And so their music has been fostered only to
give an hour or half's delight, to make a maiden blush or gently smile, and
" so to bid good-night."

The Japanese
Musicians.
And I have to add one more to the many paradoxes which
a study of the country's customs reveals. All the musicians have
an acutely sensitive ear. The tuning of any stringed instrument needs something more than mere practice : it demands the harmonic sense in great
perfection. The Koto, with its thirteen moveable bridges, is probably the
most difficult of all instruments under the sun, both to tune and to keep in
tune. Yet the tuning is faultless, and during the playing the slightest flaw
is detected immediately ; the left hand, busy as it always is in producing

the grace ·notes and accidentals which abound in all compositions of any
degree of difficulty, still finds time to be perpetually correcting the minutest
errors due to the inevitable slipping of the bridges. Yet the training is
far from perfect: there is no general grounding in intervals such as the
Western pupil must go through, only the special instruction in the actual
intervals necessary to the tuning. Knowledge of the interval between two
strings, and of its position in the sequence of intervals in the tuning, is
acquired by constant practice. The process of tuning the 7th and 8th
strings of *Hirajōshi* on the Koto would be indicated by the following
diagram; the 5th and 6th strings being supposed to be already tuned, the
player proceeds thus :—

In tuning the upper strings, the octave strings are always struck in the
same way. But I think that neither the constant practice nor the re-
iteration of any given interval is sufficient to account for the extreme
accuracy which is noticeable on all sides, without the addition of the natural
gift of the perfect musical ear.

A child destined for the musical profession—which is composed chiefly
of women and blind men — begins to learn the Koto when it is four
years old, and continues hard at work to the age of fourteen, by which
time all the elementary tunes have been learnt. In order to   *Musical Education.*
accomplish this result, when the child is eight years old, or thereabouts,

every day and all day is devoted to the work. This ceaseless devotion
to study of the grindstone order is characteristic of all the old Japanese
professions, and has produced that extraordinary mechanical dexterity
for which the nation is famous. "Ten hours a day for ten years" is
the initial routine of drudgery both for the painter and the musician; it
brings the students to the threshold of their professions, furnished with an
accuracy which is never afterwards shaken off: it has become their second
nature. It has, indeed, done more: except in the case of genius of a
high order it has crushed the first nature with its abundant gifts out of
existence; ninety out of every hundred artists and musicians, when the
years of study have run their course, have become the merest mechanics.
Means to achieve the required end are unknown; the end itself is studied,
and is achieved by continued repetitions. In music, scales and exercises,
studies, and all the paraphernalia with which the pupil is armed in the
West, do not exist. In painting, straight lines and curved lines, shaded
cubes and spheres, the "grounding" of drawing, are never learnt. Just as
the strokes which make the head, the breast, and the wing of the flying
bird are learnt from the master, as he learnt from his master, who had it
from the master who first invented them, so the passages of a musical
composition, with their phrasing and their graces, are learnt directly from
the teacher as tradition has handed them down to him. And as the methods
in music and art are exactly parallel, so also are the results. A new
musical composition is as rare as a new subject among the old school of
painters. Two new compositions in the course of a year is probably an
over-estimate of the rate of production; anything else that appears being
nothing more than a *pot-pourri* of old and well-worn phrases.

The course of instruction is divided into four stages; at the end of each a diploma is granted. These diplomas were formerly only granted by teachers who had received one of the degrees—Kōtō, Kengyō, or Sōroku : but latterly any of the male teachers have been allowed to grant them. The female teachers, who have largely increased in number since the Restoration, are not allowed to grant the diplomas. A school is visited once every three months by the teacher's former master, and the granting of diplomas rests with him.

The diploma examination is a curiously interesting little ceremony. In a small room in a very small house a crowd of twenty or *The Examination.* thirty persons are assembled, pupils, parents, friends. The mistress sits before her Koto, and in front of her six or seven Kotos are ranged one behind the other, step-wise, so as to leave the "above-bridge" space of each instrument clear : and there sit demurely the little maid musicians. Behind them again the Samisen and the Kokyu pupils. At the upper end of the room sits the blind professor with his Koto; in other nooks and corners the audience and the smaller pupils, who will presently play their little pieces separately. There is a pause in the day's occupation—one of those intervals of busy silence which play so important a part in the life of a Japanese day. Presently the door slides back, and a late comer enters. Is there, indeed, room for her? Yes, and to spare. She brings a tiny packet done up in paper, and tied with red and white string, which she hands to the school-mistress with a low bow. It is received with a lower bow and put away unopened in a mysterious cupboard. It is the fee for tuition; something miserably small to make so much fuss about—one *yen* for a month; or, may-be, she is going to receive her diploma, and this is the present-fee

K

therefor. Then with many bows and smiles she finds her place upon the floor. By-and-bye the silence is again broken; the mistress says what tune is to be taken next. I. is "Roku-dan"—the "tune in six parts"—which it is the ambition of all the little maids to play perfectly. The professor strikes the first string; the pupils adjust the ivory *tsumé* on their fingers and begin to tune. The blind man listens, striking the note on his Koto occasionally to help—listens patiently, immovably, but with acute sensibility written on every line of his intelligent face, while the teacher points out the pupils who are still out of tune. At length the professor is satisfied. Then comes the second string, an easy falling fifth—from the dominant to the tonic, if my analysis of the scale should prove correct. All the pupils know this interval well; the professor tunes his last, verifying what they have done. And so from the second to the third, the third to the fourth, till a slow sweep over all of them tells that the thirteen are in perfect tune, and the blind listener is satisfied. Finally, with the privilege which their degrees permit, the professor and the mistress lower the first string an octave, a dignity which fills some of the listeners with awe, and with an ambition that by-and-bye they may be permitted to do likewise. Then all being thus patiently made ready, the piece begins; first in solemn cadences, gradually quickening through the six parts, the divisions indicated by a slight pause and a *forte* beat on the first and second strings, till it works up to a quick time. And through the parts the leading ideas are woven in the meshes of a hundred graces and quaintnesses, which the Western stave will not hold, in the ripple of beats on two strings, and sweeps, and Æolian slides, and "waves coming and going," with a skill worthy perhaps of a better cause and more perfect, fuller-toned instruments, but woven with a constructive skill of a high order:

a skill which reveals a purpose distinctly followed to the end. At last the time slackens, gradually, as befits a close : a long sweep ending with a weird vibratory sharp long-suspended,—the Japanese cadence,—then the final note long dwelt on : heads are bent over the Kotos : the performance is over. The professor expresses satisfaction ; his attention has been almost painfully acute ; but he has no grave faults to find ; the teacher points out one or two places where greater accuracy is necessary, one or two pupils who need more practice. And then a little child of five, whose arms are hardly long enough to reach across the Koto, toddles out of the crowd, puts minute *tsumé* on her fingers, and, with the help of mother sitting beside her, goes through her little performance, and receives her little meed of praise and encouragement.

A girl should be ready to receive her first diploma two years after she has passed the infantile stage and begun the regular course—that is to say, when she is about eleven or twelve. By that time she has learnt to tune her Koto, and to play accurately about a dozen pieces. Many do not go beyond this, but are content to become the ordinary musicians of the tea-houses ; but for those who intend to become regular professionals, many and great difficulties lie beyond.

On receiving the first diploma—*omoté no yurushi*, the " front licence "— five *yen* is paid to the teacher, together with a present of *seki-han*—boiled rice mixed with a small red bean. A present of *seki-han* is also made to the fellow-pupils. The more wealthy pupils give a dinner instead of the rice and bean present. The course includes " *Hitotsu-toya* "—the counting song, or New Year's song ; " *Saita Sakurai* "—the " Song of the Blooming of the Cherry-trees," and a great number of easy

The Diplomas.

pieces ; also a certain number of more complicated ones—*kumi*, such as "*Umegaé*"—the "Song of the Plum-branch"; and ends with "*Roku-dan*." During this first course, the fees paid for tuition are : for the Koto, one *yen* a month ; for the Kokyu or Sam sen, by reason of the greater trouble in teaching and learning, two *yen* a month. These instruments, by the way, would obviously be much easier than the Koto, both for the teacher and the taught, if a better system of teaching were employed.

The second course begins with "*Kumo no uyé no kyoku*"—the "Song of the Clouds"; and ends with "*Midaré*"—"Confusion." The pupil learns the second principal tuning—*Kumoi*—the "Cloud-tuning," so named from the "Song of the Clouds," which is the first piece learnt in it ; and also the subordinate modulating tuning—*Han-kumoi*. At the end of the course, the second diploma is granted—*naka no yurushi*, the "intermediate licence," or *ura no yurushi*, the "rear licence." The payment to the teacher for this diploma is eight *yen*, with the presents of rice and beans, or the dinner, as before.

The rigidity of Japanese professional rules is well illustrated by the fact that it would be impossible for a foreigner to obtain any instruction in the pieces written in the *kumoi* tuning until he had been through the regular course, and was entitled to receive the first diploma.

The third course begins with "*Go-dan*"—the "five-grade tune"—and ends with "*Shuyen no kyoku*"—the "Song of the Banquet." The third principal tuning—*Iwato*—is earnt, and also the subordinate modulating tuning —*Gosagari-rokuagari*. At the end of the course, the third diploma is granted—*oku no yurushi*—the "innermost licence"—the fee for which is fifteen *yen*, with the rice presents, or dinner, as before. When this diploma has been obtained, the first string of the Koto may be lowered an octave in all the tunings.

In this fourth and last course pieces of great difficulty are studied, and the remainder of the subordinate tunings are learnt. It begins with "*Ōgi no kyoku*"—the "Song of the Fan"—and ends with "*Hiyen no kyoku*"—the "Song of the Flying Swallows." When this course is finished a fee of twenty *yen* is paid to the teacher for a sign-board, and permission to use the teacher's name. The pupil then becomes a professional, and is allowed to start a school on her own account. The use of the teacher's name corresponds to the "grant of one character" among artists."

A ceremony of a peculiarly Japanese character used to be performed when this dignity was reached by men. The new professor, with his fellow-pupils, his friends, and his master, journeyed to the island of Enoshima. The Koto was borne by the pupils in procession across the stretch of sand which connects the rock with the mainland, up the village steps and the steep mountain-path, then down by the other side to the sea-lapt rocks and caves. Therein, in the darkness, before the tiny shrine at its furthest end, the latest ornament to the profession played the melody named after the island ; and in the low reverences with which his former comrades greeted his performance he received the public recognition and approval of his admission. This ceremony was last performed by Mr. Yamato, only fifteen years ago.

In the foregoing pages two points seem to be perpetually recurring— the executive skill of the musicians, and the existence of something in the music itself which shows the attentive listener that it is not void and formless, but is the product of a well-considered, though somewhat inex-

tensive and inexpansive, science. On the first I must still dwell for a space before I proceed to deal with the music and the instruments in greater detail.

I have already introduced my little friends the Koto players at their work. Their industry is but the traditional industry of the whole race of Japanese musicians, and in the old days not merely traditional, but hereditary. In the city which surrounded the Palace, in the village which encircled the Temples, there was to be found not one Flute player, nor one Shō player, nor one Koto player, but whole families : of Flute players who had received the traditions of lipping and the mysteries of quarter-tones from their fathers, and who were already busy passing them on to their sons : of Shō players who, in like manner, were handing down the rules of the difficult fingering and the art of producing the gentle inhalations which alone can make the most delicate of instruments speak true : of Koto players who were training youthful ears, as their own had been trained, in the knowledge of fourths and fifths and octaves, youthful fingers to the production of sharps and graces. From father to son this traditional knowledge had been handed down ; from father to son the process would have continued far as human thought can stretch, if — if that had not happened which so abruptly changed the current of the nation's history, and twisted it into a channel where the waters must run swiftly, and in which the slow smooth progress of tradition was impossible. These present days are too new indeed for the influence of old Japan to have been entirely shaken off, the instincts of the traditions too deeply set to be quickly killed. And so we find in many cases that the dancers and musicians of to-day are the lineal descendants, the lineal inheritors of the traditions of some

far-distant ancestor, the inventor of a dance, the singer of a song that
has not yet lost its power to please. The old Biwa player who made
the "Phœnix-voiced one" discourse to us one summer evening as he sang
of the hero who, armed *cap-à-pic*, dashed with his charger into the sea to
the rescue of his comrades, and was held by his foes too valiant to be slain,
claimed a descent from one who had learnt from one who had learnt from
another, and so for a series right up to Ichibotoké, himself of the tribe and
lineage of the Heiké clansmen. More than once in the preceding pages
the name has been mentioned of one who, though his work may-be was not
quite sublime, still has followers in his foot-tracks through the sands. This
hereditary tradition of industry it is that has made the executive art of
the Japanese, without hyperbole, the foremost in the world. If their music
were as taking to Western ears as their art is to Western eyes, assuredly
we should have heard something more of the executive skill of the musicians.
Many who would perhaps admit the existence of this skill, are disposed
to think it wasted because it is devoted to instruments unfamiliar to us,
whose gentle notes are drowned in the echoes of our own gigantic
orchestras. Wasted, too, even if its existence be admitted, because it is
devoted to a music perhaps uncongenial to our taste, whose science is
lost in the shadow of the wonderful mystery of the West. But poor though
their music be, and thin the gentle twanging of their strings, this may be
maintained against all contradicting —that the executive skill of their musicians
is of the first order, and that in this respect, all other things being, alas!
unequal, they may at least hold the candles of comparison by the side of
their Western fellows ; and in their blindness, how great is this inequality!

Did tenor in the West ever sing to waterfalls night and morning through the freezing months of snow? or Western player play through the dark dawns of mid-winter till the icicles hung from his Flute; or through the fierce midday heats of summer till he was literally bathed in the sweat of his brow? Surely not. Yet this was but a small part of the drudgery of the Japanese Temple musician's early years. The *Kan-geiko* was the winter practice, when he rose at four during the thirty days of the *Kan* season— January 5th to February 6th—and worked for three hours without even the slender warmth of a hibachi to cheer him; and the *Gebuki* was the summer practice, devised in Kyoto for the special training of flute-players—the word means literally "summer-blowing"—lest their yielding to the heat should mar the grace of summer festivals. And all the year through, from morning to night, work; three hours' lesson every day, and practice the rest for as many hours as the day would yield, with a public examination six times a month.

From the age of ten to fifteen the lessons were confined to the reading of the Bugaku books, and mastering the difficulties of intonation. At fifteen the hereditary instrument was taken in hand, instruction being given either by the father himself, or by a member of the orchestra under the surveillance of the father. Visible progress was effected by the end of three years; after five years the pupil took a place in the orchestra on the lesser occasions. After the age of twenty-one, when he had satisfied the local examiners, he was sent to Kyoto to receive the higher training for two years, in order to qualify for the final certificate of proficiency, which enabled him to take his position in the orchestras of the public Sōgaku and the sacred Azuma-asobi. At Kyoto instruction was sought in the schools of the great monopolists, either in the Chinese Biwa, the Chinese Koto, or in singing, according to the student's fancy. Once in ten years only the pupils were excused this journey to Kyoto. By Imperial dispensation a musician was sent from Kyoto to the other Temples, to conduct the examinations and grant the final certificates. At the age of sixty a pension for long service was received, and the succession devolved on the son. The tradition of the profession was that if work was begun betimes, proficiency might be reached at thirty years of age, and extreme skill at forty : but by fifty the skill was passing away, and it was time to begin to think of moving off the stage and making room for others.

The hereditary office of the Temple musicians at Kyoto is of very great antiquity ; at Nikko it was founded by Iyemitsu, the third Tokugawa Shogun, where, in 1617, he founded the Temple to the memory of his ancestor the first Shogun, Iyeyasu. In the selection of his musicians from the Kyoto and other bands, he was assisted, as in all other things, by his chief adviser, the Abbot Tenkai, named after his death Jugen Daishi, the Temple to whose memory stands on the wooded summit of a hill over-looking his master's shrine.

Twenty hereditary musicians were established on the new foundation. They were divided into three classes : the "Nanto," those who had originally come from Nara, and whose duties were specially connected with the ancient Kagura ; the "Kyoto," and the "Tamoji," those who had come from Kyoto and Osaka respectively, and who were specially in charge of the Bugaku performances. Other music was shared by the three classes equally.

Their pay was at the rate of thirty-five *koku* of rice annually, paid half in money and half in kind ; and *fuchi*, a daily allowance of rice for

L

five persons. Roughly estimated, this was about equivalent to 150 *yen* a
year, at that time amply sufficient for a comfortable livelihood.

Their chief duties consisted of : first, the occasional performances of
the *Hi kyoku*—the "secret music "—in other words, music of the highest class,
which was a sealed book to all who had not obtained the final certificate
of proficiency ; secondly, the performances of the Bugaku dances which
were given on important celebrations ; thirdly, the " Azuma-asobi," a very
sacred dance, the music of which is said to have been received from heaven
by a descendant of Jimmu Tenno : it is now performed before the sacred
emblems on the two great festivals at Nikko.   To be included in the
orchestra of the " Azuma-asobi " was the summit of the Temple musician's
ambition ; thirteen only out of the twenty were specially selected, and received
extra remuneration in kind, three hundred bags of rice being distributed
among them : and lastly, the Sōgaku, public performances of orchestral
music only, which were held in the Temple on the first, fifteenth, and
twenty-eighth of each month ; and also on the festivals of the *Gosekku*—the
seventh of the first month, the third of the third month, the fifth,
seventh, and ninth of the fifth, seventh, and ninth months respectively.

If these duties were light the most rigid accuracy was expected in
the performance of them, entailing constant practice during leisure hours.
Recruits to the profession have now to acquire their art as they best
can.   The rigour of the old rules is relaxed, and the polished proficiency
which it produced is no longer expected.   Temple musicians have fallen on
evil days : their number reduced, their gorgeous costumes faded, their hats
of black lacquered paper or of quaintly-shaped gauze somewhat battered
and the worse for wear and non-repair, the gold ornament on the heads of

the Shōs passing almost out of recognition : nothing but the long-lived Flutes and Hichirikis improving as the years pass by : themselves, not endowed with such perpetual life, withering old men, ekeing out a precarious livelihood, supplementing a pittance of about six *yen* a month by performing small services in the Temples and engaging in other trades.

Temple music never greatly appealed to the people ; an audience was always quite superfluous ; it was in great part an offering to the Gods who gave it, and was self-sustaining. But in these days, when ancient glories are left to fade, and there is no money to renew them, and little desire even to repair them, the spirit of the song has fled, the energies of the musicians have withered with their fingers ; they practise no longer, and their performances have become slovenly in the extreme. They themselves are full of apologies, something more in their case than the customary Japanese formula of politeness ; their shortcomings and mistakes must be forgiven, they are quite conscious of them : they cannot be helped, even though the honourable European who deigns to give them audience should, as he certainly will—-this without trace of irony—detect them.

PART II.

THE JAPANESE SCALE.

THE JAPANESE SCALE.

SYNOPSIS.

Current statements as to the nature of the scale—Meaning of the expression "different scale"—The scientific ratios—Chinese intervals —The "bearings" of the scale—The fifth of China and of Pythagoras—"Tunings" and "scales" — The sequence of notes in the Japanese scale — The normal tuning — The gaps in the tuning — The two missing notes—Harmonizing Japanese music—The double pressures.

Tunings of the Japanese Koto—Tunings of the Chinese Sō-no-koto, and of the Bugaku-biwa.

"Hirajōshi" and its variations—"Akébono"—"Kumoi" and its variations—"Han-Kumoi"—"Iwato"—"San-sagari roku-agari"—Conclusions as to the structure of the tunings, and as to the keys on which they are based—Pentatonic character of the music—The key sequence; principle of the bridge changes—Transposition—The equal temperament system of the Japanese—"Saita-Sakurai" in three keys in string notation, and on the stave.

The Chinese scale: ritsusen and ryosen: analysis of the tunings of the Sō-no-koto.

Pitch—Time—Harmony—Form: the Dan and Kumi of Yatsuhashi; analysis of "Umegae"; analysis of "Rokudan"; analysis of "Matsuzukichi" and "Kasuga-mode."

General conclusions: the relation of Japanese to Chinese music — The modern music of Japan: general characteristics of the music: its intervals and phrases: its structure.

"Hitotsu-toya" harmonized—"Saita-Sakurai" harmonized.

I APPROACH the difficult question of the Japanese scale, or rather the expression of the basis of Japanese music in terms of the Western art, with much diffidence, for two reasons. First, because very positive statements as to the nature of the scale have already been advanced which

I think need criticism : and secondly, because it is impossible to deal with a question which is so fundamental in its nature without appearing to dogmatize : and, although the conclusions at which I have arrived are the result of as much research and examination as I was capable of conducting, I would avoid as far as possible all semblance of dogmatic utterance. The assertion that the Eastern scale so far resembles the Western, that for all practical purposes they may be treated as identical is, I think, sufficiently startling ; t could not be advanced otherwise than as my own belief : it must be for others more deeply versed in the science of music to determine whether the grounds of that belief are sufficient to warrant it.

The first of the statements alluded to is very authoritative. " Like the scale of mediæval Europe it has for its chief peculiarity a semitone above the tonic." This statement seems to be based on the opinion of a Japanese expert, Mr. Izawa, which is discussed in the following paragraph. But beyond this, I can find no authority to support the view. If we apply the ordinary meaning to the terms used, it means that the scale of Japan is not five-toned ; but that there is a diatonic scale, in which the semitones, instead of occurring as they do in the diatonic scale of the West, between the 3rd and 4th, and 7th and 8th, fall between the tonic and the 2nd, and the 7th and 8th. Assuming the first and fifth strings of the Koto, which are tuned in unison, to be C$\sharp$, the sixth string will be D, in the normal tuning *Hirajōshi*. I suppose therefore that C$\sharp$ is intended to be the tonic, and we should get the diatonic scale of Japan composed in the following way:—

$$C\sharp, \ D, \ E, \ F\sharp, \ G\sharp, \ A\sharp, \ B\sharp, \ C\sharp.$$

This is the scale of C$\sharp$ minor with a flat second. Any other note taken as the tonic gives notes which do not exist in the normal tuning of the Koto : and even this arrangement gives the fourth Koto string as A$\sharp$ instead of A. And then there are the two notes E and B$\sharp$, which are not given by the open strings, to be accounted for.

The second statement is to be found in Mr. Izawa's Report on Music published in 1883. " In the tuning called *Hirajōshi*, the 1st and 5th string, being in unison, are taken as the Tonic ; the 2nd string is tuned as the Fifth, the 3rd as the Fourth, the 4th as the Third below the tonic, and the 6th string is the Fourth above the tone last obtained, or minor Second from the tonic * * *. But if we assume the 2nd string to be the tonic, then the relations of the several tones will stand in the following order, which is essentially the same as the natural minor scale."

The order of notes referred to is:—

$$F\sharp, \ G\sharp, \ A, \ C\sharp, \ D, \ F\sharp.$$

In his second assumption, therefore, Mr. Izawa would seem to indicate the possibility of a similarity between the scales of the East and the West. But his Report does not follow up the assumption, nor does he examine into the reason for the large gaps between A and C$\sharp$, and between D and F$\sharp$. The weight of his authority is, as I take it, in favour of taking C$\sharp$ (the first and fifth strings) as a tonic; but whether of a pentatonic, or of a diatonic scale, I am somewhat in doubt.

Then there is the broad general statement that the Japanese scale differs from the European scale, which has passed into a conversational formula. Its currency has relegated Japanese music to the limbo where all is chaotic: has helped to stamp it as a concourse of weird sounds, and therefore not worth a moment's consideration.

Before examining the structure of the scale, it is necessary to determine what the expression "different scale" really means. This much, I think, may be taken for granted, that the fact that the same notes recur, though at a different pitch, as sound gradually rises, is instinctively and universally recognized. It seems also to have been known universally and at all times, that half the length of any sound-producing body, whether string, pipe, or wooden tablet, produces the same note in a higher range, the "octave" as we call it in the West. The octave, with the intervening notes, is obviously therefore the basis of all scales, and the variation in scale will depend on the variation of the intervening notes. Now, if the sound-distance between the lower and higher notes of the octave be divided in one system of music into twelve equal parts, and in another system into thirteen, it is obvious that we have two different sets of notes, two different chromatic scales, and consequently the diatonic scales of the two systems will differ radically. Campanology gives us examples of such different scales, and I believe the octave in the Arab scale is divided into twenty-six notes. If, however, two systems divide the octave into the same number of notes, and if the sound divisions are equal, then the notes of the two systems

M

are identical, and their chromatic scales are identical. The diatonic scales may, however, vary.

This, I know, is most unscientific. The chromatic scale did not precede in construction the diatonic scale, but followed it. The octave in the West is not divided into twelve intervals whose ratios are identical. In the Pythagorean scale the ratios of two semitones ($\frac{256}{243}$) multiplied together give more than the ratio of the full tone ($\frac{9}{8}$); and conversely the square root of the ratio of the full tone gives less than the ratio of the semitone. In the diatonic scale there are both major tones ($\frac{9}{8}$) and minor tones ($\frac{10}{9}$), and the semitones used between the third and fourth, and seventh and eighth ($\frac{16}{15}$), are larger than the Pythagorean semitone by a "comma" ($\frac{81}{80}$). And even those who do not much care for ratios and complicated calculations, will not fail to remember from the earliest years of their musical instruction that the "black notes" on the Piano do double duty for sharps and flats; that A♯ and B♭, for example, are both represented by the same note which scientifically is neither: mathematically, because the result of multiplying the ratio of the preceding interval by the ratio of the semitone is not identical with the result of dividing the ratio of the succeeding interval by that semitone ratio.

I introduce this parenthesis to put myself right with science. The point I wish to emphasize is that for practical purposes these slight differences are disregarded. For the question of disregarding small differences is important, because the question now before us is the comparison of Japanese and Western music from a practical rather than from a scientific point of view. Seeing that the basis of European music is neither the scale of Pythagoras nor the scientific diatonic scale, but the eminently practical equal temperament scale of the Piano the question is whether the ratios of the intervals of the Japanese scale are sufficiently near to the ratios of intervals in the diatonic scale in use in the West to enable us to disregard the differences: whether it is possible to put Japanese music on to the Western staff, and play it on that most scientifically inaccurate instrument, the Piano, without altering its character very perceptibly. Reverting to campanology for a moment to illustrate my meaning, it is common knowledge that it is often quite impossible to put the music of a peal of bells on to the Piano. Is it the same with Japanese music?

My own experience is that practically these differences may be disregarded, but the idea has been much criticized since I ventured to express it before the Asiatic Society of Japan in 1891. This criticism has, I think, rendered necessary a certain amount of rudimentary explanation.

I think that I may now safely revert to my original heresy of the equal intervals, and to the convenient idea of treating the diatonic scale as a sequence of notes selected from the chromatic scale.

Speaking then very broadly, the Chinese scale, from which the Japanese has descended, is made by dividing the octave into twelve equal intervals, and so also is the Western scale. These intervals are called in Chinese, *ritsu. Primâ facie,* therefore, they correspond to the Western semitones.

The origin of the twelve Chinese *ritsu* is given, mythologically, thus: "When in the year 1000 B.C., Wantai, Emperor of China, established music, he found out the composition of sound in the following way. His servant Leyling, who was a natural musician, went one day into a deep glen and cut some bamboo into twelve lengths. He did this because the number 12 governs all human affairs: thus there are 12 months, 12 signs, and so forth. On blowing through these pieces of bamboo he found that some had strong sounds like heavenly thunder, and some were gentle and of a wavelike murmuring, and some were metallic, others wooden, and others earthy. Then he named them, *Ichiotsu, Dankin, Hyōjō, Shōzetu, Kamu, Sejō, Fushō, Ōshō, Ranshō, Banshiki, Shinsen, Jōmu.*"

A series of bamboo Pitch-pipes is used for determining the sound of the twelve Chinese semitones, but they are scientifically obtained on the thirteen strings of the Koto from the three fundamental intervals of the fourth, the fifth, and the falling fourth: or, taking the thirteen strings of the Koto to represent an octave of semitones, the interval of the fourth will be represented by an interval of six strings, and that of the fifth, by one of eight strings, the first and last strings inclusive. The Japanese terms for these intervals are:—*jun-roku,* "the upward six"; *jun-pachi,* "the upward eight"; *gyaku-roku,* "the downward six." The addition of the two semitones, or the intervals between three strings, to *jun-roku,* which makes *jun-pachi,* and subtraction of them from *jun-pachi* to arrive at *gyaku-roku,* is called in both cases *san-bun son-yeki.*

The "bearings" of the scale are obtained by tuning the 1st and the 6th strings to a fourth, the 1st and the 8th to a fifth, the 8th and the 3rd to a falling fourth: and then the remainder of the notes come by using the fifth and the falling fourth alternately in the following way:—

1st	to	6th	.	fourth	— *jun-roku*	— C	to	F.
1st	,,	8th	.	fifth	— *jun-pachi*	C	.,	G.
8th	,,	3rd	.	falling fourth	— *gyaku-roku*	— G	,.	D.
3rd	,,	10th	.	fifth	— *jun-pachi*	— D	,,	A.
10th	,,	5th	.	falling fourth	— *gyaku-roku*	— A	,,	E.
5th	,,	12th	.	fifth	— *jun-pachi*	— E	,.	B.
12th	,,	7th	.	falling fourth	— *gyaku-roku*	— B	,,	F♯
7th	,,	2nd	.	falling fourth	— *gyaku-roku*	- F♯	..	C♯
2nd	,,	9th	.	fifth	— *jun-pachi*	— C♯	..	G♯
9th	,,	4th	.	falling fourth	— *gyaku-roku*	— G♯	..	D♯
4th	,,	11th	.	fifth	— *jun-pachi*	— D♯	,.	A♯
11th	,,	6th	.	falling fourth	— *gyaku-roku*	— A♯	,,	F. (E♯.)
6th	,,	13th	.	fifth *(octave)*	— *jun-pachi*	— F	,,	c.
1st	,,	13th	.	octave	——	— C	,,	c.

Here we arrive at a most important stage of our inquiry. We find in the Japanese scale, first, an octave divided into twelve semitones; secondly, the relation of these semitones determined on a principle which is the same as the familiar principle of the "bearings" of the Western tuner.

There seems, further, to be no doubt that this system has not been borrowed from the West, as might be supposed, but has always existed. In the description of the Koto, it has been suggested that the reason why thirteen was finally determined on as the number of its strings, was to enable all the thirteen notes to be produced on the open strings of one instrument when they were required. And as a means of testing the tuning of an instrument, a second Koto is often set with its strings tuned to the chromatic scale on this system.

I have so far assumed, for the sake of convenience, that the Eastern intervals *jun-roku* and *jun-pachi* are identical with the Western "fourth" and "fifth." This identity must now be tested. We have very precise evidence as to how the fifth was obtained. It was given by a string two-thirds of the length of the string from which the fifth was to be taken; and this, it need hardly be said, is the string-length which gives the perfect fifth of Pythagoras, and of the diatonic scale. The books, so far as I am aware, do not give the string-length of *jun-roku*; but with *jun-pachi* established, the task of comparison is simple.

The falling fourth is obviously used as the fifth inverted, giving the octave lower than a note actually given by taking the fifth from the last note, in order to bring the required note within the compass of the octave. Instead, therefore, of "falling fourths," in the above table, we may substitute fifths, and we get the complete series of thirteen notes by a continuous succession of intervals, each represented by a ratio of ⅔, the string-length of each note being two-thirds of the length of that of the preceding note : that is to say, the thirteen notes of the Chinese chromatic scale were obtained in precisely the same way as the thirteen notes of Pythagoras may be obtained by a succession of perfect fifths. The reduction of the notes into the octave compass leaves an untrue falling fourth between the eleventh and sixth strings, the sixth string being already tuned. We may, therefore, use the Western nomenclature to signify the notes of the Chinese scale, as they are used for the Pythagorean scale.

The "different scale" of Japan, then, if it exists, exists because different notes have been selected from those which have been selected in Europe to form its diatonic scale. From the same chromatic scale it is possible to construct many different diatonic scales. In Western music there are three in common use ; the major, the ascending minor, and the descending minor.

There is, however, one more previous question to be determined : what is the meaning of the word "scale"? It is a natural and continuous sequence of sounds. Continuity, or the absence of breaks, is essential. The chromatic scale is such a sequence. But the ear accepts the tone as a unit of natural progression just as much as the semitone ; that is to say, it does not feel the omission of the intermediate note. But with a larger interval than a full tone it is at once conscious of an omission. A sequence that has any larger interval than a full tone is not natural, and does not satisfy the condition which the definition of "scale" implies ; but any sequence which is composed of tones and semitones does. If this were not so, not only the six notes of the Koto should be called a scale, but also the three notes of the Samisen, the three notes of the Kokyu, the four notes of the Biwa, would be the scales of those instruments respectively ; this is obviously a misuse of the word. These are tunings, not scales.

As it is important to keep the idea of the scale perfectly distinct from the "tuning" of the strings of an instrument, so also is it important not to confuse the notes of the scale with the prevalent intervals which are frequently noticeable in national music. For example, the augmented second is a prevalent and characteristic interval in Hungarian music. But the inference that the augmented second forms part of the Hungarian scale is not necessarily warranted.

Let us now see what the sequence of notes is on which modern Japanese music is based. Now one thing at least is certain : whatever the scale may be it must contain all the notes which are to be found on the open strings of the normal tuning of the Koto. It may contain more, but it must contain these. The mediæval European scale, alluded to above, is therefore put out of the field at once because it has A♮ in its composition instead of the A♯ of the Koto. The question then arises, does this normal tuning of the Koto, to which we must confine ourselves for the present, express the full scale of Japanese music ? The notes are five in number, and taking the pitch of the second string to be represented by F♯ on the Piano, these notes are C♯, F♯, G♯, A, D. Now there is no reason, on the face of it, why the Koto strings should not, like those of the Violin, be tuned to selected convenient notes of the scale. The height of the bridges does not admit of the strings being raised by pressure more than a full tone, but the gaps are not sufficiently great to need more than this to fill them in ; assuming, of course, that there are some notes to fill in.

But even supposing that the gaps are not filled in in this way, are we to assume that because these two notes are not used, therefore they do not exist in the scale : that the scale is limited to the notes of *Hirajōshi*, and that it is consequently what is called a five-tone scale ? I see absolutely no reason for it. We have only to turn to the Yamato Koto to have this idea at once dispelled. Its six strings are tuned to the major triad of the tonic and the minor triad of the second of the Western diatonic scale : that is to say, the seventh of the scale only is omitted. Reverting, however, to the modern Koto, if the gaps which exist in its tuning exist also in the scale, the music which is built on such a pentatonic scale must refuse to recognize the existence of any notes to fill them in : it must refuse them, that is to say, in its science : the musician must not feel the want of them, nor be conscious of their existence : and further, if they are introduced, the trained musician will feel not only that they are out of place, but that if they are used in harmonizing his national music its character will be gone.

Let us assume that the existence of two notes in these two gaps is probable, the question arises, what are these notes? It is legitimate now to refer to the diatonic scale of the West for a suggestion, but only on one hypothesis, which is important: it is, that the five Koto notes are to be found in our diatonic scale sequence. Now the notes F♯, G♯, A, C♯, D, will be seen to form part of the scale of A major, or of F♯ minor descending. I assume, as before, the pitch to be F♯ for convenience of argument: but even without definite names to the notes, we get, starting from the second string, the following order of intervals:—

2nd string	to	3rd string	.	.	full tone
3rd „	to	4th „	.	.	half tone
4th „	to	5th „	.	.	major third
5th „	to	6th „	.	.	half tone
6th „	to	7th „	.		major third
2nd „	to	7th „	.		octave

The use of the terms "tones" and "thirds" is, I think, justified, since the fundamental basis of the perfect fifth has been established.

Now if we divide each major third into the two full tones of which it is composed we get the following result:—

2nd string	to	3rd string	.	full tone
3rd „	to	4th „	.	half tone
4th „	to	5th „	.	full tone / full tone } major third
5th „	to	6th „		half tone
6th „	to	7th „		full tone / full tone } major third
2nd „	to	7th „		octave

This sequence of intervals is the sequence of the descending minor diatonic scale of the West.

The suggestion is inevitable that between the fourth and fifth strings of the Koto normal tuning there is a note in the Japanese scale which is a full tone from both; and that there is a similar note between the sixth and seventh strings. Taking the pitch as before, these notes would be B and E: and, if they are legitimate, we get the perfect Western scale.

Now I have a certain amount of evidence to show that these two notes
are legitimate, and may conveniently, though not accurately, be called the
"missing notes" of the modern national music.   This evidence is of two
kinds : the statements of a Koto teacher of the old school who knows
nothing of any other music ; and those of Mr. Yamasé Shōin, a professional of the highest rank, who has, however, come under the influence
of Western music.

After many conversations with my teacher, and after seeking the information in many various and devious ways to avoid error or even doubt,
she told me that she felt, and always had felt, that there was a note
between the fourth and fifth strings, and one between the sixth and seventh.
What these notes were she did not know, nor had she any means of finding
out ; for above all things it is important to remember that a "scale," as
such, had no meaning to her.   It is important, too, to explain that a
Japanese is not taught music in the broad sense of the term ; she learns
only the music of her special instrument.[12]

I then took the Kokyu, and avoiding everything in the shape of a
leading question, I played A, A♯, B, C, C♯, several times, both in and out
of order.   She selected B as the note between A and C♯ ; and in the same
way she selected E to come in between D and F♯.   The full scale of
A major as I then played it to her satisfied her completely ; more than
this, she picked it up rapidly, and played it with evident pleasure.   Avoiding
the intricacies of our minor scale, I told her to begin on F♯, and substitute
A♯ for A♮, and so on ; we then had the scale of F♯ major, and pleasure
still more evident.   Finally we went to the Piano, and when I had told
her about the black notes and the white notes, she proceeded to fumble
out the diatonic scale for herself or any note I chose to start her on.
Our lessons thenceforward invariably terminated with a little scale-playing
by the old lady on the Piano.

It was possible, however, to go a step further.   If the scale is what I
assume it to be, if these are really "missing notes," yet another test must
be satisfied.   If a melody should be harmonized it must not lose its
character.   With such tunes as I have harmonized—two examples of which
are given at the end of this Part—I have not found the character altered
in any way : and what is more to the point the many Japanese to whom
I have played them have agreed with me in this opinion.   Obviously here

I could appeal to a larger body of witnesses. On account of the presence of, to us, awkward and unaccustomed intervals, I find much of the advanced music very difficult to harmonize satisfactorily. But this, as musicians will recognize, is beside the present question.

Yet another matter has to be mentioned as pointing in the same direction. My teacher told me more than once that the second string is the "fundamental" note, and that it is regarded as such when they tune down to it, as from the dominant, from the first string. The difficulties attending accurate interpretation, caused not only by the language but by the absence of sufficient musical knowledge in the teacher herself, made it difficult for her to explain exactly what she meant by "fundamental," but it was evident to my mind that she had some idea in her head as of a key-note.

The next point has, I think, great value. It will be observed in the scheme of strings and notes, given below, that the scale of A major lies between the fourth and the ninth strings. But as the minor predominates in Japanese music, the relative minor, F♯, lying between the second and the seventh strings, seems to be indicated as the prevailing scale. This is confirmed in a remarkable way by the popular New Year's Song—"*Hitotsu-toya*"—which not only permits the full scale of F♯ minor to be used in harmonizing it—including the use of the sharp seventh, E♯, of the ascending scale—but in its variations recognizes the essential difference between the minor and the major; this points to the existence of a fundamental idea of scale and key corresponding to the fundamental idea of Western music.

1st string	. .	C♯ in unison with 5th.
2nd ,,	. .	F♯
3rd ,,	. .	G♯
4th ,,	. .	A
"missing note"	.	B
5th string	. .	C♯
6th ,,	. .	D
"missing note"	.	E
7th string	. .	f♯
8th ,,	. .	g♯
9th ,,	. .	a

and so on.

N

Mr. Yamasé has supplemented my own observations in the following manner: my only reason for not putting his views first is that I cannot quite decide whether they have not been to some slight extent tinged by his studies of European music.

He says that the second string, F#, has always been considered as the fundamental note in the tuning, not only of *Hirajōshi*, but of all the others: F# and the C# of the first string being constant throughout. As to the missing notes, he says that certainly the existence of some others has always been known, because the Koto tunings were founded on the Chinese chromatic scale, and also because they could be produced on the Kokyu. And, further, that B and E are distinctly pointed to as the missing notes of the scale, because in tunes written in *Hirajōshi*, the "double pressure" (*nijū oshi*), when it does occur in the classical music, invariably occurs on the 4th string—A—giving B: and on the 6th—D—giving E; and also on their octave strings respectively, the ninth and the eleventh.

Notes of the *Hirajō-hi* tuning, with the two notes used in the Classical Music.

It does not appear, however, that the use of these notes is frequent: in the examples of elementary classical music which I have given — "*Umegae*" and "*Rokudan*"—neither B nor E occurs once. These notes are found, however, more frequently in the more advanced music.

We now come to the other tunings of the Koto, which are set out in the diagram on page 92.

No. 1 is *Hirajōshi*. No. 2 shows the first string lowered an octave, as used by the professionals. No. 3 is a variation of *Hirajōshi*, the last three strings being changed from D#, F, G#, to F#, G#, C#, the 10th and *kin* strings giving an octave: hence this variation is called *Kin-jū*. In No. 4 we have another variation of *Hirajōshi*, all the strings being raised a fifth, thus giving three additional notes above the normal *kin* string, A, C#, D#. It is not very clear why this upper D is sharpened. It is probably introduced either for the sake of brilliancy, or for the sake of the extra semitone, the 12th string sharpened giving D# when wanted. This tuning, as it gives a higher range of notes, enables pieces to be played an octave higher; when two Kotos are used together one of them is usually tuned to it, the performers playing in octaves. In the upper part, which is taken by the leader, innumerable graces and complicated little variations are introduced on to the melody, much in the manner of the Treble part of duets on the Piano, which add considerably to the charm of the performance.

In No. 5 we come to the first new arrangement of the strings. It is called *Akébono*, and springs directly out of *Hirajōshi;* differing only in the sharpening of the 6th and 11th strings, and introducing E on the 7th and 12th, instead of F♯. If anything were wanting to complete the proof that the five notes of the Koto do not by themselves constitute the Japanese scale, it is supplied by this tuning, which has six notes: the five notes of the normal appear in it, together with the missing E.

The notes belong to the scale of E major, giving it with the omission of one note only, B, which can be produced by the double pressure on the 4th and 9th, in the same way as B is supplied in *Hirajōshi*. It seems, however, that the tuning is not used in this way, though it has an important position in the scheme of keys. The most frequent pressed notes are simple pressures on the 4th, 7th, and 9th, giving A♯ and E♯; and, in consequence, the scale of F♯ major. This is in accordance with the Japanese idea which connects *Akébono* with *Hirajōshi*.

No. 6 is *Kumoi*, the "cloud" tuning, which, next to the normal tuning, is in most frequent use, and is ranked by the Japanese as the second principal tuning. It is so named because the first tune learnt in the tuning is "*Kumo-no-ye*"— the "Song of the Clouds." The 3rd and 4th strings are G and B, instead of G♯ and A, in the normal; the 8th, 9th, and 13th being tuned to the octaves respectively. These changes give a different character to the music, suggesting the introduction of a fresh key; and analysis bears out this suggestion in rather a curious manner. The five notes, D, F♯, G, B, C♯, form part of the Western scale of D major, or B minor descending; and applying the same process of reasoning that was adopted in the case of *Hirajōshi*, the missing notes are E and A. We do, in fact, get a fresh key. But perhaps the most interesting feature of this new key is that, in what I may call the Koto expression of it, the same two notes are omitted, the fourth and the seventh. This enables Koto music to

TUNINGS OF THE JAPANESE KOTO.

Strings :—1   2   3   ·   5   6   7   8   9   10   11 (*to*)   12 (*i*)   13 (*kin*)

1. **HIRAJŌSHI.**

2.   "   [For those who have received the third grade diploma: the first string is lowered an octave in *Hirajōshi* and all other tunings.]

etc.

3.   "   (*kin jū*).

4.   "   (raised a fifth).

5. **AKÉBONO.**

6. **KUMOI.**

7. **SAKURA.**

8. **HAN-KUMOI.**   [HIRAJŌSHI.]   [KUMOI.]

9. **IWATO.**

10. **GO-SAGARI ROKU-AGARI.**   [IWATO. . . . . .]   [KUMOI . . . .]

The three principal tunings are underlined.

SPECIAL TUNINGS.

11 **KURAMA-JISHI.**   Afterwards changing to **HIRAJŌSHI** by lowering the 6th and 11th strings a semitone.

12. **HIRAJŌSHI.**   With the 4th and 9th strings raised a semitone, and afterwards lowered to the normal.

TUNINGS OF THE CHINESE SŌ-NO-KOTO
AND OF THE
BUGAKU BIWA.

be easily transposed from *Hirajōshi* to *Kumoi*. The relation between the Koto tuning and the Western scale is borne out in precisely the same manner as before ; the missing notes can be supplied by double pressure on the sixth and eighth strings ; and these are the double pressures which are invariably used in classical music written in *Kumoi*.

Notes of the *Kumoi* tuning, with the two notes used in the Classical Music.

I do not know how far the knowledge of the relation which exists between *Kumoi* and *Hirajōshi* extends—probably a very little way. Even so perfect a Koto musician as Mr. Yamasé, who has always more than suspected the existence of such an intimate relation between *Hirajōshi* and the Western scale as I have pointed out, had not observed that the relation between *Kumoi* and that scale was precisely identical. Although transposition is very rarely resorted to, if at all, he knew that the *Hirajōshi* music could be transposed into *Kumoi*, and as a matter of fact he could transpose it without the slightest difficulty. But directly we get below the highest rank of professional, the rote-teaching of the music steps in to prevent the acquisition of such knowledge, because all the tunes would have to be learnt twice over.

I mean that a tune, "*Hitotsu-toya*" for example, is learnt by the numbers of the strings, thus—9, 9, 10, 9, 10, 10, etc., and not as we should learn it, by the intervals of the scale, thus—3rd, 3rd, 5th, 3rd, 5th, 5th, etc. Transposing on the Japanese system involves, therefore, the learning of a fresh sequence of strings : thus in *Kumoi*, "*Hitotsu-toya*" would be written thus—6, 6, 7, 6, 7, 7, etc.

No. 7 is *Sakura*, a variation of *Kumoi*, made by introducing a higher note on the thirteenth string, B instead of G. In this respect *Sakura* holds to *Kumoi* a relation much resembling that of *Kin-jū* to *Hirajōshi*, the twelfth and thirteenth strings being at an interval of a fourth. The eleventh and twelfth strings are, however, not raised as in *Kin-jū*. On the same principle of nomenclature *Sakura* might be called *Kin-ku*, the new thirteenth string giving the octave from the ninth.

We now come to a curious tuning called *Han-kumoi*, or "half-*kumoi*." It is a mixture of *Hirajōshi* and *Kumoi*, the first seven notes being in the normal, the next five in the "cloud" tuning. The G♯ of the thirteenth string is probably to be explained in the same way as the D♯ of *Hirajōshi* when raised a fifth—(No. 4).

At first sight, and, indeed, for some time after, this arbitrary tuning seems to upset any idea that may have been formed from what has gone before as to the existence of a Japanese scheme of scale and key. The explanation of its existence is, however, simple. It is sometimes necessary to change rapidly from *Kumoi* to *Hirajōshi*—to modulate, in fact, from F♯ minor to B minor ; and this complex tuning enables it to be done with greater ease, by reducing the number of bridges which require to be shifted.

It is possible to play in the key of B minor in the *Hirajōshi* tuning : the G naturals can be produced by a simple pressure on the second string and its octaves, the seventh and twelfth, the B's by double pressure on the fourth, and its octave, the ninth. And, similarly, it is possible to play in F♯ minor in the *Kumoi* tuning ; the G sharps being produced by simple pressure on the third string, and its octaves, the eighth and thirteenth, and the A naturals by double pressure on the same strings. But the use of double-pressures instead of open strings is obviously to be avoided if possible : when the transition from one key to the other occurs during the progress of the piece, the change in the tuning is effected by rapid bridge changes made with the left hand. In order to effect the change from *Hirajōshi* to *Kumoi* the bridges of the third, fourth, eighth, ninth, and thirteenth strings would have to be moved. But to avoid this complicated change, and further, to avoid the danger of the changes not being perfectly in tune, the lower strings are often kept in *Hirajōshi*, the upper half in *Kumoi ;* and hence has sprung the tuning *Han-kumoi*. When the piece is alternating rapidly, as often happens, between the two keys, *Hirajōshi* can be played on the upper strings (tuned to *Kumoi*) by using the necessary pressures ; and so *Kumoi* can be played on the lower strings (tuned to *Hirajōshi*) by the same means. But when the piece settles down into either key, the number of bridge changes is not only reduced by half, but they can be easily and accurately made, because their octave strings are already in tune. Thus, if there is a long passage in *Hirajōshi*, the eighth and ninth bridges only have to be shifted in order to tune the strings to the octaves to the third and fourth ; and similarly, if the piece settles into *Kumoi*, the third and fourth bridges only have to be shifted in order to tune the strings to the octaves of the eighth and ninth.

The thirteenth string is kept to the G♯ of *Hirajōshi*, probably in order to save the trouble of an additional bridge change, so that the sweeps over the strings in that tuning may be accurate ; and also because the G♮ of *Kumoi* can be produced by pressure on the twelfth string.

No. 9, *Iwato*, the third important tuning, springs out of *Kumoi* by lowering the fifth string a semitone and raising the sixth a tone. The constant quantity of all the tunings, the C♯ and F♯ of the first and second strings, is preserved, but the first string is seldom used in *Iwato* music. As the first and the fifth strings are normally in unison, the former never holds a very prominent position in Koto compositions ; it is seldom used, except to reinforce the fifth, or to get a slightly different intonation when the two are struck consecutively by the second finger and thumb, or in the *Kaki* beat ; and in this latter case, from the nature of the beat, accurate tuning is not absolutely essential. *Iwato* is constructed on precisely the same principle as *Hirajōshi* and *Kumoi*, the notes giving, as before, a major and a minor scale ; G major and E minor, the fourth and seventh of the diatonic minor, being omitted as before. And, again, not only are these missing notes supplied by double pressure on the eighth and tenth strings, but these are the double pressures which are invariably used in classical music written in *Iwato*.

Notes of the *Iwato* tuning, with the two notes used in the Classical Music.

No. 10, *Go-sagari roku-agari*—the "lowered fifth and raised sixth"—is a mixed tuning, developed out of *Iwato* and *Kumoi*, and used to facilitate rapid transitions between those tunings, in the same way as *Han-kumoi* is used to facilitate transitions between *Kumoi* and *Hirajōshi*. It is, however, constructed in the inverse order to *Han-kumoi*, the first to the seventh strings being in *Iwato*, and the eighth to the twelfth in *Kumoi;* the G♯ of the thirteenth being retained as before. All the changes indicated in the preceding explanation of *Han-kumoi*, as occurring on the third and fourth and eighth and ninth strings respectively, occur in *Go-sangari roku-agari*, on the fifth and sixth and tenth and eleventh strings respectively.

Some authorities give the eleventh string in this tuning as E, instead of D. I think, however, that the symmetrical construction of the scheme of tunings points inevitably to D as the proper note.

These are all the regular tunings; in addition, however, there are some special tunings, which have no distinguishing names, being only used for certain tunes which require a note not in the regular tunings; they frequently revert to the regular tunings during the progress of the piece. Thus, No. 11 is the tuning for the piece "*Kurama-jishi*." It is written in *Hirajōshi*, but D♯ is frequently used in the early part; the sixth and eleventh strings are therefore tuned up a semitone for convenience. After a time, however, D♮ reappears, and at given points the bridges of the sixth and of the eleventh strings are moved back to their normal positions, and the tuning reverts to *Hirajōshi*. In the same way in No. 12, the fourth and the ninth strings start tuned to A♯, and are afterwards lowered to the normal A♮ of *Hirajōshi*. [13]

And now, what are the conclusions which this analysis forces upon us?

In the first place, that "scale" and "key" were principles with which the early founders of Eastern music were familiar; they possibly did not so thoroughly understand them as to be able to reduce what they knew into transmissible thought. But what they knew was precisely what we know in the West—that music must be built upon a systematic sequence of notes; their science gave them the same natural notes that Pythagoras employed; and their instinct led them to a sequence which is the sequence of the West, thus confirming in a remarkable manner our somewhat arrogant assumption that we alone had received nature's revelation. They knew that music acquired brilliancy when played upon a range of notes of a high pitch, and solidity and profundity when their range was lowered. Above all, they knew that the major and the minor modes are in the main the natural exponents of the two chief emotions of mankind, gaiety and sadness.

But I think they knew, or after a time discovered, more. The whole scale could not be put on to an instrument with only thirteen strings

Gzzz;

without curtailing its compass. The dimensions of the Koto, therefore, imposed upon them very practical limitations in determining how the scale should be rendered upon it. Certain notes of the scale had to be selected for the "open notes," leaving the other notes to be produced by pressures when wanted. Why the fourth and seventh of the minor scale, or the second and fifth of the major, were omitted there is no tradition to tell us, and, as we shall presently see, there is a curious divergence on this point between the Japanese and the Chinese tunings : but a very unscientific suggestion may be made.

A feature of the oldest music of Japan, that of the Yamato-Koto, was a scratch of the plectrum over the six strings : this seems without doubt to have been the origin of the modern sweep with the *tsumé* over all the thirteen strings. It was obviously necessary that this characteristic feature of their music should be melodious, and the first thing that strikes the student of Japanese music is the melodiousness of the sequence of the strings. The open strings of *Hirajōshi* give an *arpeggio cadenza* which would have rejoiced the heart of Mendelssohn, who revelled in such æolian music,

But this selection of notes led inevitably to the construction of melodies built on the selected notes, the open strings, alone. The composers of the severe classical school might use pressures and double pressures, and build their music on the full scale ; but the songs for the children and the melodies of the lighter sort came inevitably to rest on the notes of this æolian *arpeggio*, and on those alone : and so, as it seems to me, came into being the *Koto-uta* of the present day, for which I can find no name less graceful than *arpeggio-music*. In the West, Scarlatti had once done the same as a *tour de force ;* he had built the subject of his " Cat's Fugue " upon the five black notes of the Piano. And, indeed, our own Bugle music supplies an apt analogy, its melodies being built on the notes of the common chord. Even to the easy classical music, of which I have been able to give two examples, the tuning imparted a pentatonic character. The simple phrases of " *Umegae* " and " *Rokudan* " are constructed entirely on the open strings, and there seems to be very little doubt that, from their frequent use musical thought among the Japanese runs almost entirely up and down these five notes, obviously limiting its powers of expression.

A more scientific suggestion may, however, be made. The evolution of the seventh of the scale far away up in the altitudes of the natural musical sounds is so curious that it is not surprising that it should be called the last discovered note: it is not surprising that it should have been omitted in the Eastern tunings. Now, if we take a two-stringed instrument with frets, such as the Gekkin, tuned to a fifth, it is obvious that, as the same fret does duty for both strings, if the seventh is omitted on the first string the fourth will be omitted on the second string. The diagram showing the Gekkin frets on page 170 will make this clearer. In this way, two-stringed instruments tuned in fifths being very common, it seems probable that the fourth and the seventh have become intimately connected. It is possible that a very similar reason accounts for the omission of the third in the Chinese *ritsusen* tunings of the Sō-no-koto: two-stringed instruments being also occasionally tuned in fourths.

I may here allude to the "cyclical tetrachord" theory which has been advanced in opposition to my own theory of the similarity of the Western and Eastern scale-systems. (Dr. Knott, "Transactions of the Asiatic Society of Japan," vol. xix., pt. II., p. 373.)

If we start from the fifth string of the Koto we get C♯, D, F♯ -a fourth, and G♯, A, C♯ - a fourth. The fascinating "tetrachord" is almost immediately suggested, for the arrangement of notes in the two groups is identical, the intervals being a semitone and a major third. By assuming that the gaps in the "tetrachords" can be filled in in a variety of ways, and by putting them together "disjunctively," the complete Dorian mode sequence is obtained, and the conclusion is somewhat rapidly arrived at that Japanese music is based on the "Dorian mode." The contention is supported by reference to many pieces of Japanese music which finish on C♯: some of them, indeed, end on G♯, and in harmonizing "*Hitotsu-toya*" the last chord must undoubtedly be the common chord of C♯; but this is, as it seems to me, nothing more than the ending on the dominant so common in old "round" music.

The cyclical form of the tuning, though exceedingly curious and interesting, cannot outweigh the other evidences which point to a sequence of notes in the scale identical with that of the Western diatonic scale. That scale itself, it need hardly be said, is also based on the "cyclical tetrachord" system, two similar tetrachords being put together "disjunctively."

But the suggestion in the preceding paragraph seems to afford a perfectly simple explanation why a cycle of intervals should be found in the tuning: the frets of the Gekkin, with its two strings tuned to a fifth, repeated on the second string whatever intervals the first string gave, only a fifth higher.

We may now take one more step forward. It needed musical capacity of the most primitive order to understand that a lower pitch could be given to *Hirajōshi* by moving all the bridges down a degree; but a greater contrast was desired—the lowering the pitch a fifth—than could be effected practically by moving all the bridges.

Before determining what science it was that enabled them to do it, it is necessary to describe the system which the early Japanese musicians adopted in order to effect this lowering of the pitch in the simplest possible way. If the right hand on the Piano is on the notes C, E, G, we are in the key of C major; by moving the thumb a semitone higher we have the notes C♯, E, G, and the key of D major: and so on. And so it is on the Koto: if the right hand covers the third to the seventh strings, the notes which fall under the fingers are from G♯ to F♯ in *Hirajōshi*; but in *Kumoi*, after making the two bridge changes, the notes are from G♮ to F♯, and we are in a different key.

Now, if *Kumoi* were an entirely new and independent tuning, with no inherent relationship to *Hirajōshi*, a fresh arrangement of the strings might have been devised for the open notes; another *arpeggio* might have been invented, with a fresh series of melodies; but the Japanese musicians—and I think here I may use Japanese as distinct from Eastern—deliberately set themselves to make the new arrangement of the strings dependent on the notes of the *arpeggio* established by *Hirajōshi*, and yet it was to bring a new series of scale-intervals into the normal position of the hand.

Without scientific knowledge they devised a re-arrangement of strings giving the same *arpeggio* cadence in a different order and in a different key. Again they had a harmonious sequence composed of the notes of the diatonic scale with the second and fifth of the major, the fourth and seventh of the minor, omitted. The *arpeggio* of *Hirajōshi*, starting from the second string, is made up of the following intervals of the major scale: the 6th, 7th (below the tonic), 1st, 3rd, 4th, 6th, 7th, 8th, etc.; of *Kumoi*, it is the 3rd, 4th, 6th, 7th (below the tonic), 1st, 3rd, 4th, 6th, 7th, 8th, 10th, etc., and therefore, although if we start from the same string, the full *arpeggio* sequences of the two tunings sound very differently to the ear, if we start in *Hirajōshi* from the second, and in *Kumoi* from the fourth string, we hear precisely the same sequence of intervals, but in *Kumoi* pitched a fourth higher.

Yet again we find the same principles applied to the evolution of a third principal tuning—*Iwato*—formed out of *Kumoi* in precisely the same way as *Kumoi* was formed out of *Hirajōshi*. Again the pitch is lowered a fifth and a fresh set of intervals brought into position, and again we find the key of the sub-dominant taken the next in the order of the scale sequence. *Iwato* gives E minor with its relative G major, the fourth and seventh of the minor, or the second and fifth of the major, being omitted as before. The C♯ of the first string remains constant, as has already been explained; the F♯ of the second string has become the second of the minor scale, its importance being correspondingly diminished. The *arpeggio* of *Iwato* is : 7th (below the tonic), 1st, 3rd, 4th, 6th, 7th, 8th, etc. And, again, if we start on the sixth string we hear precisely the same sequence of intervals as before, and again pitched a fourth higher than in the preceding tuning. With *Iwato* the sequence of scales ends, the key of its sub-dominant requiring F$\sharp$, which would involve an alteration in the fundamental second string.

The principle of the bridge changes in the consecutive tunings is revealed in the name of the mixed tuning—*Go-sagari roku-agari*—used for facilitating the transitions between *Iwato* and *Kumoi*. *Iwato* is obtained from *Kumoi* by lowering the fifth string a semitone, and raising the sixth a full tone ; or, in terms of the diatonic scale, lowering the leading note and raising the tonic. And this is precisely the way in which *Kumoi* was obtained out of *Hirajōshi*: the leading note G$\sharp$ of A major is lowered to G$\natural$; the tonic A is raised to B. In Japanese terms this application of the principle might be called *san-sagari shi-agari*.

Here, then, we have the practical factor by which the sequence of scales was made ; and if the first and second strings were not constant, it might be applied for the formation of all the other scales ; thus,

> For making *Kumoi* from the normal, lower the 3rd string a semitone, and raise the 4th a full tone ;
>
> For making *Iwato* from *Kumoi*, lower the 5th string a semitone, and raise the 6th a full tone ;
>
> For making the next scale from *Iwato*, lower the 7th string a semitone, and raise the 8th a full tone ; and so on.

So much for the principal tunings. But the group of scales clustered round the C$\sharp$ and F$\sharp$ of the first and second strings is not yet quite accounted for. There is the normal F$\sharp$ minor with its relative A major ; secondly, there is the scale of the sub-dominant B minor with its relative D major ; thirdly, again the scale of the sub-dominant E minor, with its relative G major. But these three relative major keys are, as far as I have been able to trace, quite ignored. Probably owing to the important position held by the second string, and for other reasons with which musicians are familiar, the transition from grave to gay, of the method of which the variations of "*Hitotsu-toya*" are good examples, is better effected by using the keys of the tonic majors, instead of the relative majors. Thus, the major corresponding to the F$\sharp$ minor of *Hirajōshi* would be F$\sharp$ major, and not A major. For short transitions the simple pressure on the fourth, and its octave, ninth, would be sufficient; for longer cheerful compositions, however, *Akébono* was invented. This tuning, and other variations already noticed, are not recognized by the Japanese as *chōshi*—the equivalent for "scale": they are called *te*; and it is not necessary in these subordinate tunings, invented purely for convenience, to look for diatonic scale notes. Thus, in *Akébono* there is no difficulty about the A♯ of the fourth string : A♯ is producible at pleasure by pressure, but an open string A♮ is convenient for those short transitions into the minor, and *vice versâ*, which are so frequent in Japanese music.

The key of B major has not been specially provided for *Kumoi* in the same way, but the possibility of making such a tuning, if it were required, seems to be admitted. Curiously enough the E major, which, as I have already pointed out, exists in *Akébono*, would serve the purpose for *Iwato ;* but, as it would involve transposing the piece on to a different order of strings, it is not so used.

We have now a perfect sequence of keys :—

A major	*Hirajōshi*	not used.
F♯ minor	*Hirajōshi*	
F♯ major	*Hirajōshi*	by pressure on the 4th and 6th strings, and their octaves, for short transitions, or
	Hirajōshi	by bridge changes (No. 12) for longer passages, or
	Akébono	for pieces in the major key.
D major	*Kumoi*	not used.
B minor	*Kumoi*	
B major	*Kumoi*	by pressure on the 6th and 8th strings, and their octaves.
G major	*Iwato*	not used.
E minor	*Iwato*	
E major	*Iwato*	by pressure on the 8th and 10th strings, and their octaves ; or
	Akébono	by transposition of strings : not used.

Transitional tuning for *Iwato* to *Kumoi*—*Go-sagari roku-agari.*
    ,,   ,,   for *Kumoi* to *Hirajōshi*—*Han-kumoi.*

The sequence principle is, therefore, a fall of a third from major to minor
alternately; or from major to major, and minor to minor, a fall of a fifth.
And this is precisely the backward scale-sequence of Western music.

The principle of the Western scale-sequence backward is, a fall of a
fifth and flatten the seventh; the principle of the Japanese sequence is
the "*sagari-agari*" rule, already explained. The principle of the Western
sequence forward is, a rise of a fifth and sharpen the fourth; the principle
of the Japanese sequence the other way about, that is to say, from *Iwato*
to *Hirajōshi*, is obviously the reverse of the rule just given, and might
be called "*agari-sagari*."

And now we come to the last point of the enquiry: how, with Pythagorean notes, were they enabled to obtain the transposition of the pentatonic
sequence by means of this simple system of bridge-changes? In the Piano
illustration which I used above, the relation of E to G in the C major
sequence C, E, G, is identical with the relation of E to G in the D major
sequence C♯, E, G. In the corresponding Koto illustration the relation of
C♯ to F♯ (5th to 7th strings) in the *Hirajōshi* sequence G♯, A, C♯, D, F♯,
is identical with the relation of C♯ to F♯ (5th to 7th strings) in the *Kumoi*
sequence G, B, C♯, D, F♯. Further, the full sequence of intervals in *Kumoi*
is identical, as I have shown above, with the full sequence of intervals in
Hirajōshi, just as the full sequence on the Piano of D major is identical
with the full sequence of C major.

Yet we know that if the notes of the Piano were tuned in C major,
either to the Pythagorean or the diatonic scale, the "wolf" would be heard
when the C was changed to C♯ in the above illustration: we should not
get the true interval E to G of the scale of D major. We know now
that the fundamental Chinese scale was made of "fifth upon fifth," like the
Pythagorean: and we must know, therefore, that we should find somewhere
a Chinese "wolf" by preserving intact the interval C♯ to F♯ both in the
Hirajōshi and the *Kumoi* sequences: and yet it is absent, for perfect tonal
transposition is possible. There is but one conclusion. The Japanese do
not use, on the Koto at least, the Pythagorean notes. They have tempered
them in some way; and seeing that transposition is possible, the principle
which governs the Koto must be the principle which governs the Piano.
That principle is "equal temperament"—and this was invented in Japan,
unless Yatsuhashi went to Desima and learnt it of the Dutch, about the

year 1620, one hundred and twenty years before Bach wrote his Forty-eight
Preludes and Fugues for the "well-tempered Clavier."

This is not a mere question of theory; it is supported by facts derived
from the Japanese themselves. I cannot say that my suggestions either agree
or differ from theirs, for they have none to offer. The fact that the highest
professionals know something, but that something very dimly, of the relations
between the tunings, does not affect the truth of the statement that the
theory of their scale is absolutely lost. But the practical test is that, if
the theory is sound, transposition on open strings should be possible on
the Koto. And the best of the musicians can invariably transpose melodies
in the three principal tunings of *Hirajōshi, Kumoi,* and *Iwato.*

Dr. Knott, in his paper already alluded to, bears me witness, if unwittingly, at least in a most
remarkable manner. He has built his "tetrachord" theory on the notes of the Gekkin; and he
tells us of three several instruments — the Chinese Gekkin, the Nagahara Gekkin, and the
Keian Gekkin. Each of these instruments, assuming the frets to have been glued on to the
necks of the instruments with an intense accuracy, and to have remained in position, gives a
different scale. This is the scheme of vibrations:—

FRET.	CHINESE.	NAGAHARA.	KEIAN.	MAJOR SCALE.	
0	300	300	300	300	(*doh*)
1	335	337	333	337·5	(*ray*)
2	365	368	371	375	(*me*)
3	400	398	397	400	(*fah*)
4	443	446	447	450	(*soh*)
5	505	500	497	500	(*la*)
6	598	598	595	600	(*doh*)
7	681	671	667	675	(*ray*)
8	815	797	800	800	(*fah*)

More valuable testimony to the theory I have ventured to propound it would be impossible
to receive. The difference between the upper B♯ produced by twelve fifths and the upper C
produced by seven octaves is the celebrated "Pythagorean comma." It has been eliminated
and distributed over the various intervals of the scale—in one way, under the "unequal temperament" system, which gave a truer scale in a few keys and a terribly untrue scale in a
great many; in another way, under the "equal temperament" system, which gave no true
scale in any key, but the same scale in all keys. So this table of vibrations (assuming the
frets in position accurately) shows us the different schools of Gekkin players endeavouring
each in its own way to distribute the "Chinese comma" over the other intervals of the scale.

Neither the Chinese, nor the Nagahara, nor the Keian school seem to have thought a true octave essential : the two former were satisfied with two vibrations too few, the Keian with five ; and so through the other intervals.

On any of these Gekkins transposition is obviously impossible; on the Koto it is possible. We have on the Koto parallel keys, as we have on the Piano. It is to be noted that an extremely sensitive ear should be able to appreciate a difference between two notes two vibrations apart, sounded independently. Putting my own evidence out of the question, I am certain that if the keys were not parallel, the difference of the tonal relations of the intervals after the very simple bridge changes from *Hirajōshi* to *Kumoi*, and from *Kumoi* to *Iwato*, had been made, could not have been passed over by the extremely sensitive ears of the Japanese musicians who have transposed melodies for me.

I now give the tune "*Saita Sakurai*" in the three tunings, side by side, in string notation, and on the Western staff in the keys of F♯ minor, B minor, and E minor.

SAITA SAKURAI.

[Read down the columns and from right to left. The figures indicate the strings to be played.]

IV.			III.			II.			I.		
I	K	H	I	K	H	I	K	H	IWATO	KUMOI	HIRA-JOSHI
i	10	kin	9	i	10	4	7	5	6	9	7
to	9	i	8	to	9	3	6	4	6	9	7
10	8	to				4	7	5			
9	7	10	9	i	10	5	8	6	7	10	8
			10	kin	to						
			9	i	10	4	7	5	6	9	7
4̄5	7̄8	5̄6							6	9	7
4̄5	7̄8	5̄6	9	i	10	4	7	5			
9	i	10	8	to	9	3	6	4	7	10	8
			7	10	8	2	5	3			
4̄5	7̄8	5̄6				1̄2	1̄2	1̄2	1̄2	1̄2	1̄2
4̄5	7̄8	5̄6	6	4	7						
9	i	10	6	4	7	8	to	9	8	to	9
			7	5	8	8	to	9	8	to	9
8	to	9	6	4	7	7	10	8			
			6	4	7	6	9	7	7	10	8
9	i	10	7	5	8				6	9	7
8	to	9				7	10	8			
7	10	8	8	6	9	6	9	7	7	10	8
			9	7	10	5	8	6	6	9	7
6	9	7	10	8	to	1̄2	1̄2	1̄2	5	8	6
									1̄2	1̄2	1̄2
7	10	8	i	10	kin	8	to	9			
			to	9	i	8	to	9	8	to	9
7	10	8	10	8	to	7	10	8	8	to	9
6	9	7	9	7	10	6	9	7	7	10	8
5	8	6							6	9	7
9]	7]	5]	8	6	9	7	10	8	7	10	8
4]	2]	1]	9	7	10	6	9	7	6	9	7
			10	8	to	5	8	6	5	8	6

SAITA SAKURAI.

In *Hirajōshi* (F♯ minor). [Written an octave higher than the *Koto*.]

In *Kumoi* (B minor). [Written to actual notes of the *Koto*.]

In *Iwato* (E minor). [Written an octave higher than the *Koto*.]

THE CHINESE SCALE.

THE discussion on the Japanese scale should have been preceded by an examination into the Chinese scale ; but for many reasons the difficulties of getting at it, of deciphering the sounds, and of transcribing any music which could explain it, are infinitely greater even than in the case of the Japanese scale. The tunings of the Sō-no-koto are set out in the table given on page 93 ; it is printed so as to face the tunings of the Koto, for convenience of comparison.

In the first place, there are two terms which require explanation—*ritsusen* and *ryosen*. They are interpreted by Japanese musicians who are familiar with Western music as equivalent to the minor and major respectively, and I think this interpretation is accurate. The words indicate, as is usual with things which go in couples and are the complement of each other, the " male " and " female " elements : the major is represented by the male, *ryosen ;* the minor by the female, *ritsusen ;* and it will be seen that each of the tunings has the two modes. The name of the tuning is generally applied to the *ritsusen* mode, but in two cases the corresponding *ryosen* mode has received a separate name—*Taisiki*, the *ryosen* of *Hyōjō ;* and *Suijo*, the *ryosen* of *Ōshiki*.

All the tunings are composed of five notes with their octaves, and, as before, these five notes may be taken as indicative of the scale and key of the music based on them ; though it is beyond my power to apply the tests of harmony and transposition as in the case of the Japanese tunings.

The six-note tuning of the Japanese—*Akébono*—does not appear to have its counterpart in China. A careful examination reveals a constant difference between the notes of the *ritsusen* and *ryosen* of the different tunings ; one note only is changed, and that is lowered a semitone from the minor tuning to the major.

Thus, in *Hyōjō*, the five notes of the *ritsusen* mode,
F♯, G♯, B, C♯, D♯, become F♯, G♯, A♯, C♯, D♯,
in the *ryosen* mode : the B falling to A♯.

In *Banshiki:*

F♯, G♯, A♯, C♯, D♯, become E♯, G♯, A♯, C♯, D♯:
the F♯ falling to E♯.

In *Ōshiki:*

F♯, G♯, B, C♯, E, become F♯, G♯, B, C♯, D♯:
the E falling to D♯.

In *Ichiotsu:*

F♯, A, B, C♯, E, become F♯, G♯, B, C♯, E:
the A falling to G♯.

And in *Sōjō:*

F♯, A, B, D, E, become F♯, A, B, C♯, E:
the D falling to C♯.

Now, proceeding on lines analogous to those adopted in unravelling the Japanese tunings, the five notes of *Hyōjō* appear to belong to the diatonic scale of F♯ with the third and seventh omitted. The omission of the third prevents our saying whether it is F♯ major or minor; but we may conclude that A♮, the minor third, is the missing note, because in *Taisiki,* the corresponding *ryosen,* A♯—the major third of the scale—is inserted, and the missing notes are the fourth and the seventh.

Further, the Chinese word *Hyōjō* has precisely the same meaning as the Japanese word *Hirajōshi,* both signifying "normal scale." If, therefore, the preceding assumption is true, we find the normal tuning of the Sō-no-koto is built on the same diatonic scale as the normal tuning of the Koto, but with different intervals—the third and seventh being omitted instead of the fourth and seventh. The tonic major—F♯ major—produced from *Hirajōshi* by pressures on the fourth and sixth strings, is given by the *ryosen, Taisiki;* the fourth and seventh of the scale being omitted in both.

The practical information necessary to support this theoretical view of the *Hyōjō* tuning is, however, wanting. I have been unable to ascertain whether the missing notes, A and E or E♯, are, in fact, supplied by pressure on the third and sixth strings, or double pressure on the sixth. The theory may, however, be supported inductively, for we find that the assumption holds good for the other tunings, and supports similar conclusions.

Thus, in *Banshiki:*

the notes of the *ritsusen* mode, C♯, D♯, F♯, G♯, A♯, C♯, give the scale of C♯ minor with the third and seventh omitted ; and of the *ryosen* mode, that of C♯ major with the fourth and seventh omitted : C♯, D♯, E, G♯, A♯, C♯.

In *Ōshiki* :

the notes of *ritsusen*, B, C♯, E, F♯, G♯, B, give B minor with the third and seventh omitted ; and of *Suijo*, the corresponding *ryosen*, B major with the fourth and seventh omitted : B, C♯, D♯, F♯, G♯, B.

In *Ichiotsu* :

the notes of *ritsusen*, E, F♯, A, B, C♯, E, give E minor with the third and seventh omitted ; and of *ryesen*, E major with the fourth and seventh omitted : E, F♯, G♯, B, C♯, E.

And in *Sōjō* :

the notes of *ritsusen*, A, B, D, E, F♯, A, give A minor with the third and seventh omitted ; and of *ryosen*, A major with the fourth and seventh omitted : A, B, C♯, E, F♯, A.

It would appear, therefore, that the assumption made in the case of the normal is warranted, all the other tunings conforming to the same test.

The tunings of the Bugaku-biwa also support these conclusions. It will be seen that the lowest string is invariably tuned either to the keynote or the dominant of the key to which, it is suggested, the tunings respectively belong.

The change which is constant in all the transitions from *ritsusen* to *ryosen* is the lowering of the fourth of the minor scale a semitone, apparently giving the third of the tonic major.

In the constant omission of the seventh from all the tunings the Chinese and the Japanese systems resemble each other.

Further, if the above assumptions are accurate, we get the following sequence of keys, transposing the order of *Banshiki* and *Hyōjō* :—C♯, F♯, B, E, A,—a fall of a fifth ; this is the same key-sequence as the Japanese, the backward key-sequence of the West.

But beyond this sequence of keys, and the fact that six notes of the diatonic eight only are taken for each tuning, there seems to be no connecting link between the Japanese and the Chinese tunings, and I cannot discover in the Chinese any such symmetrical scheme of construction as the Japanese tunings revealed. Above all, I have no data on which any conclusion could be based as to whether or not it is an "equal-temperament" scale.

PITCH.

ON the subject of pitch, in spite of the savour of an ancient theory which seems to attach to the statement, I am tempted to say boldly that the key of F♯ minor on the Piano more nearly renders the plaintive character of the Koto music in the normal tuning. I have used it invariably in transcribing on to the Western staff, as the other keys seem too clear and open, or too heavy and lugubrious ; and it is when I have played in this key that the Japanese musicians have agreed with my conclusions. It has, indeed, the practical advantage of avoiding the use of flats, which impede the clear rendering of the music on the Western staff, as the flat is not known on the Koto, and sharp pressures would often have to be translated by naturals.

It is not, however, necessary to rely on the old favourite idea that each key had its special characteristics. Although a pitch-pipe is sometimes used, the first string, the dominant of the scale, is tuned first, and is within limits arbitrary : for a loud singer it is tuned up, for a singer with a small voice it is tuned down. But the normal pitch of the note approximately is middle C ; I have, however, taken it as C♯. On the Japanese Flute this note lies midway between C and C♯ on a Piano tuned to Broadwood's Philharmonic pitch tuning.

For the sake of convenience of reference I have kept to the same pitch in transcribing the Chinese tunings, though I believe that the Chinese normal pitch is slightly lower than the Japanese.

TIME.

ON the question of transcription one other point remains—the time. In spite of much *rubato* and of many seeming lapses from regular and metronomical time, the beat is alternate and equal. The unequal accent of our common time seems hardly suited to Japanese music. I therefore always use ¾ time, which seems accurately to convey the idea of the *hyōshi* marks, or bars, in the example of Koto notation given on page 162.   Many of the phrase difficulties are apparent only, and are caused by the presence of innumerable grace notes, and also, I am bound to say, by the carelessness of many of the ordinary musicians.

An explanation of the complex system of Chinese time will be found on page 199, under the description of the Kakko, the small Drum used in the Bugaku orchestra

---

HARMONY.

THE statement that Japanese music is devoid of harmony is, perhaps, the only one among the many current dogmatic utterances on the subject which at all approximates to accuracy. So far as my observations have carried me there is very little ; but there is some. But, again, I have to remark that until we can examine the higher forms of Koto music our judgment must remain in suspense. My impression is, that when elaborate compositions are studied (such an one as *"Adzuma-jishi,"* for example, a name which will recall a very graceful but complicated piece sometimes heard at the Maple Club in Tokyo), we shall find a great deal more harmony than we at present imagine.   I have, however, to deal now with facts, not impressions.

The simple fact that two notes may be played together with pleasing effect is recognized by the existence of the term *awaseru*—literally "to put together" ; it is used as well for the reinforcing unison of the first and fifth strings, as for the octave which is frequently used in whole passages. Thus, in *"Hitotsu-toya,"* the first and one of the simplest of the *Koto-uta,* octave passages frequently occur. In the third variation, moreover, we find some traces of harmony : the interval of the sixth, for example, which adds vigour to the melody :—

and also that of the minor seventh, which is used with great effect and emphasis. It comes, indeed, as somewhat of a surprising refutation of the statement that no harmony exists, occurring as it does thus early in the musician's learning :—

and the interval of the seventh is also doubtless part of the chord of the minor seventh on the second : the second passage, more fully harmonized, standing thus :—

Using Western terms, the interval of the sixth is doubtless part of the common chord of the tonic, the key at the commencement of the two variations being F♯ major, and the first passage, more fully harmonized, may be rendered thus :—

The first of these two chords, the fifth string and the sharpened ninth,—I am disposed to say, as might be expected of the common chord of the tonic,—is of frequent occurrence. Thus, the phrase which commences each fragment of "*Matsuzu-kishi*" is as follows :—

a variation of the leading phrase of "*Hitotsu-toya*" in the major. The following is another example of its use, from "*Kurama-jishi*" :—

In a piece called "*Gosho-guruma*,' again, the eighth and sharpened *to* string occur in harmony, giving a major fifth :—

I cannot pretend that these few examples do more than support the limited statement that there are distinct traces of harmony in the modern Koto music. I have not unravelled the harmonies of the Chinese music, but the scheme of chords, given with the description of the Shō, on page 188, indicates that harmony, though perhaps of a crude sort, formed a very important part of that music.

FORM.

PERHAPS the most interesting fact which a study of Japanese music reveals is, that it is not formless and void, but is built on an elaborate system of construction, which, if its products were filled out with harmonies and that complicated musical verbosity which is the delight of Western musicians, would entitle it to a very favourable comparison with our own music. What Japanese music shows us is, as it were, the skeleton of construction ; and I find it a very interesting, well-knit, and cleverly-articulated skeleton.

The rules established by Yatsuhashi dealt only with the dimensions of the composition, and did not touch its interior structure ; in this matter he seems to have thought example better than precept.

The rules for the structure of Koto music, apart from the short songs, are interesting : it is divided into two classes, *dan* and *kumi*. The *dan-mono* are written in parts—"steps" or "grades"—in a severe style with connecting motives, but without a voice part. The grades are called respectively *ichidan, nidan, sandan,* and so on, and the whole piece is often named after the number of *dan* of which it is composed : thus there are pieces called "*Godan*," "*Rokudan*," "*Shichidan*," "*Hachidan*," "*Kudan*," the pieces with five, six, seven, eight, and nine steps. Each *dan* is composed of fifty-two *hyōshi* or bars : the first, however, may have fifty-four, and the last fifty. This is the case in "*Rokudan*," as will be seen from the printed version of it on the staff given on page 120, and I believe also in most of the compositions of the class.

The *kumi* are somewhat lighter in style, but are, like the *dan-mono*, written in several parts ; they are invariably accompanied by the voice. The parts correspond with the verses of the song, and are called *hito-uta, futa-uta*—"first verse," "second verse"—and so on. Each verse is divided into eight sections, and each section into eight *hyōshi.* The "verse" is, therefore, twelve bars longer than the *dan.*

As to the internal structure, or principle of composition, I have been unable to discover anything in the shape of rules or suggestions, or even analysis, in the later books, and the Koto musicians have very little to say on the matter. Ignorant of the Japanese idea, we can only look at it, therefore, with Western eyes, and to this end I proceed to analyse the piece "*Umegae*" — "The Plum Branch" — the first *kumi* which is taught to beginners. It is accurately rendered on the Western staff on pages 116, 117.

In the first place it will be noticed that it is built entirely on *kaké*, the undulations of the phrase having probably suggested its name. In the first verse this subject is given out seven times, making seven distinct phrases, which I have lettered A, B, C, D, E, F, G. Variety or colour is given by starting the subject on different strings. This sequential treatment is, in fact, a common device of contrapuntal music, where the subject often reappears a third or fifth higher or lower, and so on, sometimes modulated into another key, but as often not." The peculiar feature of the repetition of the *kaké* subject is, as is pointed out in the explanation of Koto terms, that the relations of the strings not being constant, the musical intervals composing the phrase must vary. Thus, in A (*to kaké*) and B (*i kaké*) the first interval is a second, but in E (*jū kaké*) and F (*hachi kaké*) it is a third. Finally, on its seventh appearance the subject is decapitated, having three notes only instead of five ; it is really *shichi kaké*, an octave below the *i kaké* of D.

The chief feature of the remainder of the seven sections is the recurrence of a short phrase composed of the 10th, *to, i,* strings arranged in different ways : thus, 10, *to, i ; i, to,* 10 ; *to, i,* 10 ; 10, *i, to ; i, to, i,* 10 ; and so on.

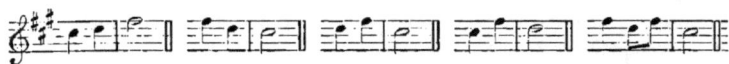

UMEGAE—("The Plum Branch").

Hito-uta—(First verse).

Futa-uta—(Second verse).

Mi-uta—(Third verse).

Yo-uta—(Fourth verse).

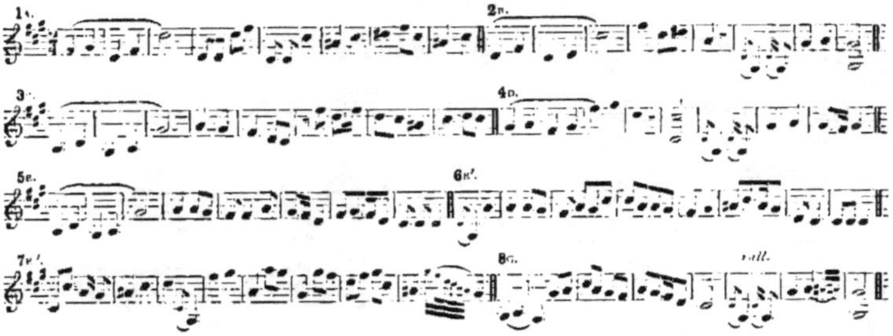

Itsu-uta—(Fifth verse).

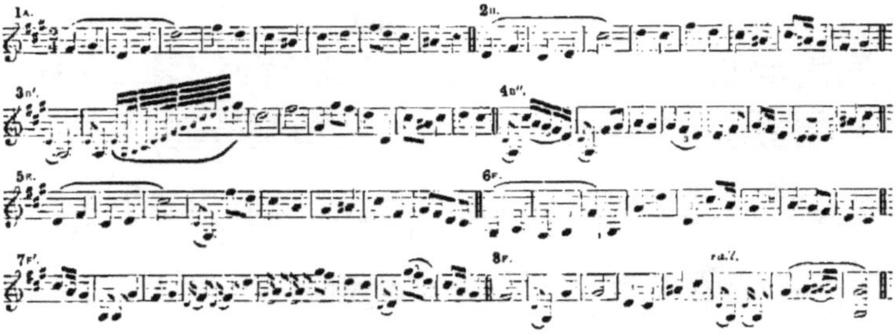

Mu-uta—(Sixth verse).

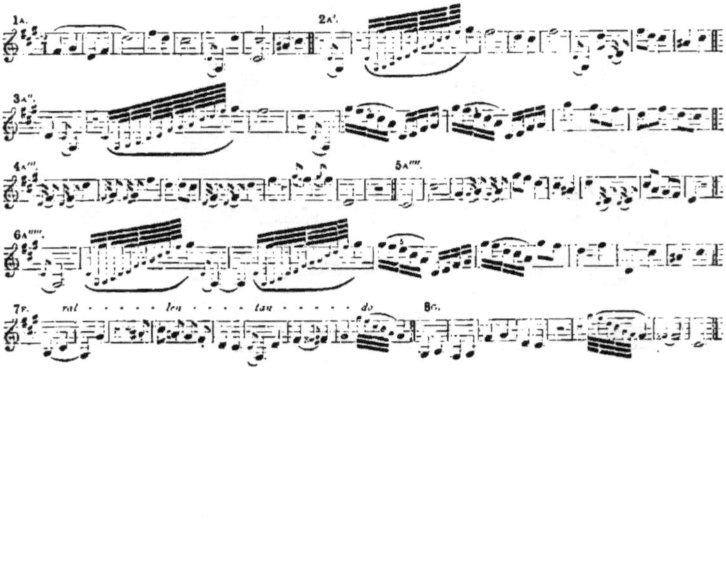

The fourth section has a second part, in which the *kaké* subject does not appear. It is written in a freer style, with more graces and slides ; it is lettered D′. The short *rallentando* close of the verse is constant in the first five variations :—

So much for the first, or chief part; we may now follow the construction through the remaining five verses. The phrase A begins all through with the subject in its normal form, *to kaké*.

Apart from the first phrase, however, each succeeding verse throws off some feature of the first verse, and specially elaborates one or more of its sections ; and, further, each verse borrows some feature from its predecessor.

In the second verse, A is identical, and B almost, with A and B of the first verse. C introduces some slight changes. D is simplified, and its second part is omitted; but E is elaborated with a second and a third part, E′ and E″, in which entirely new subjects are given out—in E′ an interesting phrase of quavers ; and in E″, an equally interesting phrase in octaves, syncopated. F and G are discarded, E″ running on into the eighth section, introducing the close by a glissade, which, however, is taken in strict time.

In the third verse, at C, *to kaké* is given out an octave lower, as *roku kaké*, a chime-like variation of the principal subject caused by the rise to C♯ on the third note instead of the usual fall. Three variations are appended to D ; the octave passage introduced in E″ of the second verse appears in D‴ inverted; and the verse terminates with G in its decapitated form, a new variation introducing the *rallentando* close.

In the fourth verse, the first four sections are treated simply, the subject being given differently in each. Two variations are attached to E ; the quaver subject introduced in E′ of the second verse, reappears in E″, varied in its second part ; and in E‴ the inverted octave passage of D‴, of the third verse, is introduced with an interesting variation in its form. F is discarded, and the verse closes with G decapitated as before, the close being introduced by a fresh quaver passage.

In the fifth verse C, D, and G are discarded; B has two variations, and F one, which is continued into the eighth section, and leads up to the close.

Finally, in the sixth verse, B, C, D, and E are discarded, a long and elaborate second part being inserted after A, which occupies five sections. This is the climax of the composition, the *namigaïshi*, most elaborate of graces, being reserved for it; it contains suggestions of many of the subordinate ideas scattered through the second parts in the preceding variations.

The composition is then closed in a sedate and dignified manner with a continuous *rallentando*. The phrase F is used concisely with *hachi kaké* decapitated. At G the *shichi kaké*, which has hitherto been decapitated before the half close, is given in full, an inversion of the phrase being appended to it; this introduces the full close to the song.

"*Rokudan*," which is set out on the Western staff on pages 120, 121, is the simplest illustration of the second class of Koto classical music, and may be subjected to a similar analysis. Each *dan* will be found to consist of two sections, the first occupying rather less than a third of the part. The sections are marked with an asterisk.

The principal subject is the following passage:—

which occurs over and over again throughout the composition, marking, in some form or other, both the beginning and the ending of all the *dan*.

This simple form is elaborated into a second subject:—

which is itself subjected to many variations, its chief characteristic being the introduction of an accidental, which is immediately contradicted on the next return to the note. The following varieties of it will be easily noticed:—

ROKUDAN—(The Six-Grade Tune).

Ichi-dan—(First part).

Ni-dan—(Second part).

San-dan—(Third part).

Yo-dan—(Fourth part).

Go-dan—(Fifth part).

Roku-dan—(Sixth part).

R

Again, a variety is introduced a fifth lower, thus :—

The introduction to the sixth part will be seen to be built up on this phrase, with the introduction of double *kaki* beats.   Finally, it is elaborated into a third subject, which occurs at the end of the first part :—

with the following variation a fourth higher, corresponding to the variation of the simpler phrase given above —

Another important feature is the phrase rising to and terminating abruptly on the major third, which is of frequent occurrence :—

Octave passages are also scattered through the parts, out of which the following rhythmical figure is made up :—

In the fifth part this is echoed immediately a fourth higher :—

Each of the first five parts is played quicker than the preceding one ; when the first section of the sixth part, which starts *allegro,* is reached, the time is gradually slackened to *andante.*

In the lighter and popular songs, the same precision of construction, and adherence to principles of form are, it is needless to say, not observed.

The two melodies, " *Hitotsu-toya* " and " *Saita-Sakurai*," printed on pages 130, 131, speak for themselves. But, before leaving the subject, it will be interesting to glance at some of the more formal of the lighter pieces : and for this purpose I have translated two into Western music, " *Matsuzu-kishi*"—" The Pine Branches" (page 124), and " *Kasuga-mōde* "—" On the Road to the Kasuga Temple " (page 125).* [13]

" *Matsuzu-kishi* " is composed of ten short phrases, of which all contain eight bars, except the fourth, which has twelve, and the tenth, which has fourteen. The remaining eight closely resemble one another—so closely, indeed, that at first hearing they seem to be precisely identical.

The theme—

occurs in all except the fifth part ; the remainder is built up of variations on this simple phase :—

and the close :—

but in every one these phrases are subjected to some very subtle change ; more especially the close, which is given with every conceivable variation of time and accent. The first bar is changed in all the subsequent parts to a short passage with the major fifth, which has already been noticed.

" *Kasuga-mōde* " is a composition of an entirely different character : it is more sparkling and more continuous, and its phrase repetitions are of a very graceful and interesting character.

---

* The chief compositions of Yatsuhashi are comprised in the following list, all of which are frequently performed at the present day :—*Umegae, Kokorozukushi, Tenkataihei, Usuyuki, Yuki-no-asa, Rokudan, Seirō, Kumo-no-uye, Usugoromo, Kiritsubo, Hachidan, Midare, Suma, Kumoi, Shiki-no-kyoku, Ōgi-no-kyoku.*

MATSUZU-KISHI—("The Pine Branches").

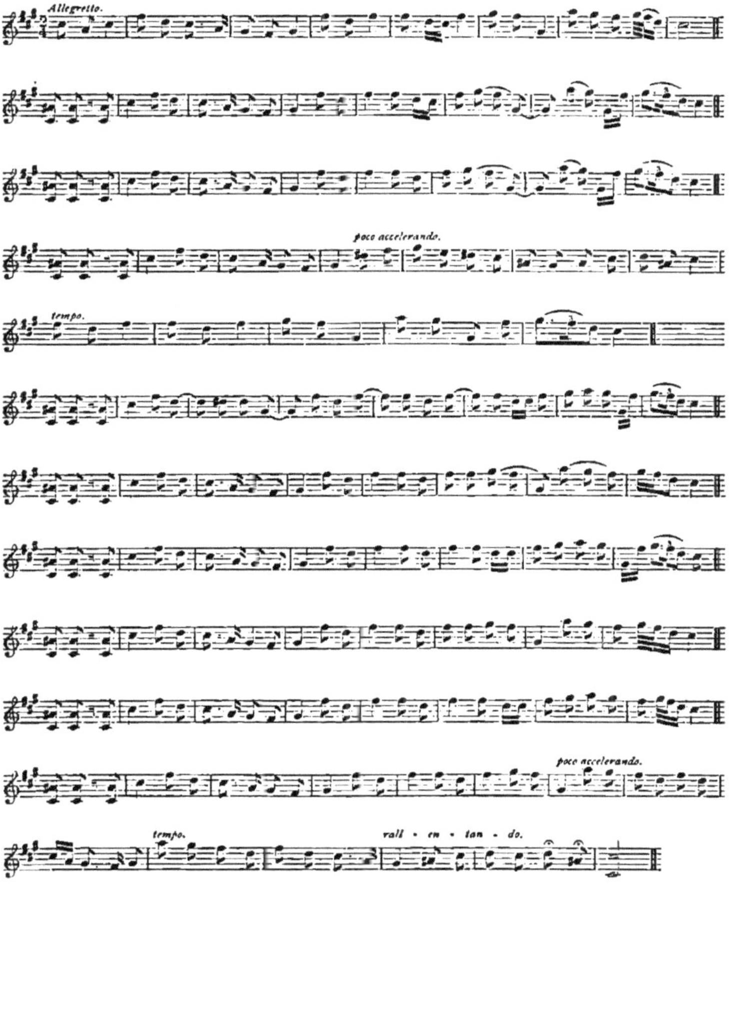

KASUGA-MŌDE—("On the Road to the Kasuga Temple").

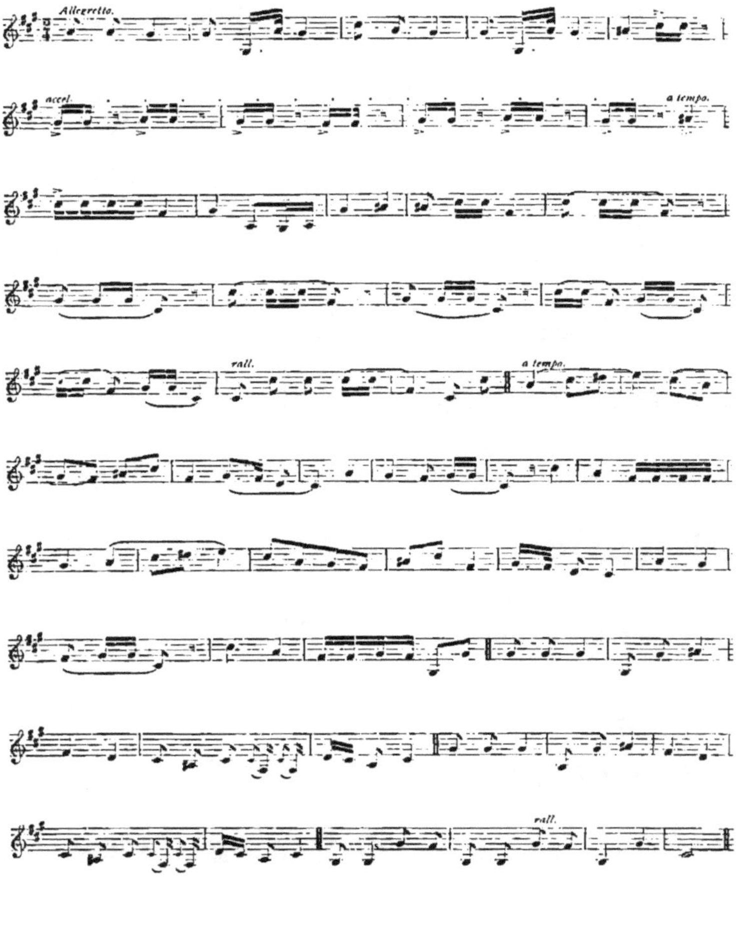

It is incontestable that at first hearing, and, indeed, after many hearings, this music leaves much to be desired; perhaps, indeed, it merits some of the epithets which have been bestowed upon it. I do not imagine that the classical examples which I have given will do otherwise than emphasize those epithets on the lips of many. But I think that they do establish at least one point in its favour; that there is, in the midst of much that is weird, a considerable amount of graceful and melodious phrase-composition, and that, though the materials are limited, an ingenuity of a high artistic order is displayed in varying these phrases and in weaving them together.

But almost all the music that we hear is, as I have indicated, pentatonic in its character; apart from the limitations it imposes, our ears are not only unaccustomed to such music, but do not very willingly get accustomed. I doubt if the absence of the seventh is very material in this respect; but the absence of the fourth has undoubtedly something to do with it. Our ears must I think, miss the phrases and sequences—"God's music," they have been called—in which the fourth of the scale holds a prominent position.

I imagine that different character in music is derived almost entirely from the prevalence of certain intervals. The Japanese themselves were probably not far wrong when they classified the different "new music" in old days according to the character of the intervals used. And so I think the most cursory analysis of this Koto music reveals two qualities, the one good, the other bad. The good—those graceful phrases I have referred to –charms us; the bad—the prevalence of awkward and ungainly intervals, and, consequently, a queer unmelodic formlessness in many of the phrases—irritates us: they are so unlike the smooth, natural sequences with which our own music abounds. Perhaps, after all, it is not surprising that in the struggle between the good and the bad characters, the victory has remained with the latter, for graceful and pretty phrases are but a poor compensation for a too prevalent ugliness.

Let it be confessed at once that such passages as these find no way to please the Western ear:—

Nor such as this—the opening phrase of "*Yatsuyo-jishi*," a piece in the *Kumoi* tuning :—

Nor are the queer drops in these two phrases of "*Umegae*" such as are likely to yield delight to the soul of the Western musician :—

But I need not accumulate instances of phrases out of which it is impossible to twist musical meaning such as we understand it; the printed examples of the music will undoubtedly furnish quite sufficient to any who care to seek for them. Nor, on the other hand, is it necessary to accumulate instances of phrases of the other kind, for they are to be found plentifully scattered, not in the classical examples which have been given, but in the more popular forms, of which "*M..tsuzu-kishi*" and "*Kasuga-mōde*" are excellent illustrations. I select the following only for the purpose of making the point clear that something at least is to be said on the other side.

From "*Rokudan.*"

From "*Umegae.*"

From "*Kurama-jishi.*"

As to the form of it, I have analysed at some length two elementary pieces of classical Koto music, one of each class, *dan* and *kumi*, because without such an analysis it would be impossible to arrive at any notion of the Japanese idea of composition. I do not imagine that every composition when subjected to the same rigorous analysis would reveal so intricate a construction as appears to exist; but when we find it in the least advanced example of the severer music, we are certainly entitled to assume that the principles of construction are not ignored in the more elaborate compositions. A complete mastery of the science of "form" must be in the East, as it is in the West, the corner-stone of all successful composition. It seems fully in accordance with the Western idea, too, that in the elementary compositions of a rigid or classical nature, the elements of the science should be easily discoverable, their clothing of phrases being only the thinnest of coverings. What, then, is the Japanese idea as we see it after our analysis? A composition built on a principal theme, constantly recurring, but in varied forms: to the principal theme, subordinate themes added from time to time, these again recurring in varied forms: finally, a gradual working up to a climax which is full of pleasant reflexion of all that has gone before; being, in fact, the themes and pretty phrases of the composition woven together.

The little popular pieces, such as "*Saita-Sakurai*," speak for themselves; and of "*Hitotsu-toya*"—indeed, it is curious that so simple a song, the very first piece of music that the children learn to hum, and the maidens to play on Koto or Samisen, contains within itself the refutation of three of the statements that are made to the discredit of Japanese music. "It is altogether unmelodious." Why, here is a little melody full of grace, catching to the ear, to be whistled, to be hummed, to be strummed, like any Western popular song. "The distinction between major and minor is unknown." And here is this tune, which, in its first variation, goes from the minor to the major in a manner which no tyro among musicians can fail to recognize. Lastly, "There is no harmony." And yet in both its variations there are most distinct traces of harmony, not elaborate, it is true, but sufficient to show that the harmonic science was not altogether unknown.

I have ventured to give these two melodies at the end of this Part, with harmonies based on these harmonic indications, and which have been received with approval by Japanese musicians who have listened to them.

And in the more elaborate popular music, such as "*Matsuzu-kishi*" and "*Kasuga-mōde*," do we not again find a reflexion of the main principle on which the classical music of Yatsuhashi was built? Themes constructed of delicate little phrases; variations with subtly reminiscent suggestions of the principal theme; and graces superadded, through which its charm is plainly visible.

Surely the Western idea does not altogether differ from this. In means for carrying it out, for inventing grander themes, for elaborating them, for beautifying them, for involving them one with the other, for mystifying the clear vision of the brain by surrounding everything with a delightful mist of sound, yes: the music of the East cannot compare with the music of the West. But again I say we must remember the few pitiful strings, the imperfect knowledge of the scale, the deficient knowledge of the capacity of some of their instruments, and then I think what has been done is a thing to wonder at and not to scoff at; and again I say we have no notion how far this modern Japanese music has gone, because we don't listen to it, and we won't listen to it, and as yet there is no means whereby we may study it for ourselves when the sliding doors have been drawn to, and the tea-house candles have been extinguished.

HITOTSU-TOYA.

Accompaniment.

First Variation.

Second Variation.

SAITA-SAKURAI.

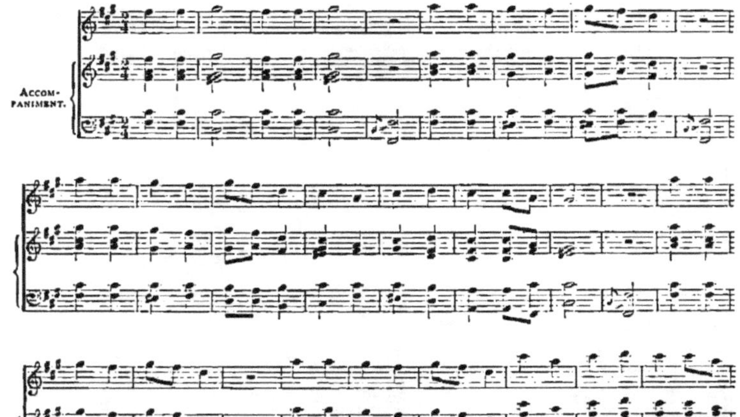

PART III.

THE MUSICAL INSTRUMENTS
OF THE JAPANESE.

JAPANESE INSTRUMENTS.

SYNOPSIS.

THE KOTO:—*Historical outline — The Yamato-koto — Diagrams of hand positions—Measurements of modern Kotos—Varieties of Kotos— General scheme of development—Technical terms used for Koto music— Koto notation—Facsimile of a page of Koto music, with translation.*

BIWAS, AND STRINGED INSTRUMENTS WITH FRETS:—*Varieties of Biwas—Measurements—*THE GEKKINS.

SAMISENS, FIDDLES, AND STRINGED INSTRUMENTS WITHOUT FRETS:—*Tunings of the Samisen — Varieties —* THE KOKYU — *Chinese Fiddles.*

FLUTES, AND BAMBOO WIND INSTRUMENTS:—*Varieties of Flutes—* THE HICHIRIKI—THE SHAKUHACHI — THE SHŌ — *Arrangement and measurements of pipes : scheme of chords.*

DRUMS:—I. *Plain cylindrical Drums*—II. *Drums with braces : scheme of Chinese time*—III. *Drums with dumbbell-shaped bodies, or Tsuzumi.*

GONGS:—*Varieties of Gongs.*

BRASS INSTRUMENTS.

THE KOTO.

THE KOTO is the chief of modern Japanese instruments. In its present form it is the last of a long series of instruments, the one developed out of the other, some with many strings, some with few, of which four principal and several minor varieties remain in use at the present day.

From what has already been said on the subject of the Kin and the Koto, it appears that this class of instrument originated both in China

and Japan, all the evidence which is available pointing to the fact that
the Yamato-koto is indigenous to Japan. The instrument in its popular
form, however, originated without doubt in China, and went through many
stages of development there. When this development was arrested, many
forms of the instrument seem to have passed into Japan, where the process
was continued.

Its form, a number of strings stretched over a long narrow sounding-
board, was the same at all periods of its existence. The principal variations
consist in the dimensions and treatment of the sounding-board, and the
method of attaching the strings to it : in the number of strings, and consequent tunings ; the minor variations, in the shape of the *tsumé*, or playing
nails, the quality of the strings, the height of the bridges, and so forth,
these last having been made in more recent times to improve the quality
of the tone. The strings, it should be said, are of tightly twisted silk,
soaked in wax ; and we find strings of different thickness, more or less
tightly twisted, and induced with a lighter or heavier coating of wax.

It seems possible to divide the numerous forms of the instrument into
three groups : first, those with one or more strings, tuned in unison or to a
fifth, attached to tuning-pegs, and played with *tsumé*, the notes being produced by stopping ; secondly, those with a fixed bridge at each end, with
many strings tuned in different ways, but without tuning-pegs, the strings
being permanently stretched, and the notes produced by stopping as before,
but *tsumé* not being used in general ; thirdly, those with a movable
bridge, or loose fret, for each string.

Before describing the many varieties of which the first two classes are
composed, some further particulars of the main group may now be given.

According to the "Outline of the Origin of the Sō-no-koto Music,"
written by Yamada Ryu, a master of the Japanese Koto, and the inventor
of the form of it in principal use at the present time, the period in which
the Kin is supposed to have originated in China is that of the Emperor
Fukki—B.C. 2000. It measured 7 feet 2 inches (one foot longer than the
modern instruments), and had only five strings. In the Chew dynasty,
150 years later, a sixth string was added ; and later still a seventh. The
early Kin remained a seven-stringed instrument for a long period, and as
such it is generally quoted in the books. It was made in two sizes, the
smaller being an octave instrument measuring 3 feet 6 inches. A miniature

THE KOTO-PLAYER
(From an old print by an artist ...)

Koto — the Han-koto — used, in old Japanese days, to form part of a traveller's luggage; and it seems reasonable to suppose that the small Kin in older times was made for the same purpose, and was called into being by the same fondness for its music. In the Chin dynasty another miniature Kin, 3 feet 7 inches long, appears to have been in vogue, and also a one-stringed instrument, Ichi-gen-kin, which disappeared from China to reappear in later times in Japan under the same name.

An endeavour to make the Kin a twelve-stringed instrument seems to have failed, probably because the need for a many-stringed instrument was already supplied by the Hitsu-no-koto, which is attributed also to the reign of the Emperor Fukki. We can only conjecture what the precise differences in construction between the Kin and the Hitsu-no-koto were, the only records being as to the number of the strings. At first, the Hitsu-no-koto had fifty; but in the reign of the Emperor Kōtei the number was reduced to twenty-five; it was again reduced by the Emperor Shun to twenty-three, "many other alterations being made at the same time." It measured 8 feet 1 inch long, by 1 foot 9 inches broad. After a time three more strings were discarded.[16]

Two further varieties are noticed in the books: the Shō-hitsu-no-koto, 7 feet 3 inches long, with twenty-five strings, and "ornamented with precious stones"; and the Chiku-no-koto, a thirteen-stringed instrument struck with a short bamboo—*chiku*. "Even the Kin," says the historian, "was sometimes struck with a stick, the idea having originated with a poet who derived inspiration from striking the strings with his pen."[17]

At the points of greatest interest in the history of Japanese music, when the thirteen-stringed Kin was finally established in China, and which of the many forms already noticed came to Japan, we unfortunately find the greatest doubt. The Chinese instrument now used for Chinese music in Japan is neither the pure Kin nor the Hitsu-no-koto, but the Sō-no-koto; and even in the sober work of so accomplished a musician as Yamada Ryu, its introduction into these islands is surrounded by angels, mountain-tops, clouds, and lovely ladies. The story of the mountain-grove has already been told. The period is given as the reign of the Emperor Temmu, about A.D. 673.

The Chiku-no-koto is the first thirteen-stringed instrument mentioned, but this again is treated as quite distinct from the Sō-no-koto. The

T

number, though as a matter of course it is connected with all other human and divine things which have settled themselves into thirteen, seems undoubtedly to have been finally determined upon because it could give the full octave of *ritsu*, or semitones, one string for each, when they were required.

Somewhere, then, in the mists of the early Chinese dynasties, about two thousand years ago, the Sō-no-koto developed out of the Hitsu-no-koto, and came to Japan with Chinese music, dancing, and the rest of the Chinese orchestra, about the middle of the seventh century. It remained the fashionable instrument of the Japanese Court for upwards of a thousand years, but was used for Chinese music alone. National music was left to the Yamato-koto—of which more hereafter—the Satsuma-biwa, and the other instruments which had gradually developed in Japan.

The development of the Japanese Koto out of the Sō-no-koto is, however, given by Yamada Ryu with the precision with which it has already been related.

The two forms in which the Japanese Koto is now found are, first, the Ikuta-koto, which developed out of Yatsuhashi's improvements; and, secondly, the Yamada-koto, in which the instrument has been brought to its highest pitch, no further development having been attempted, and none indeed seeming possible. The Sō-no-koto remains for use when the old Chinese music is performed.

It has been impossible to give more than the barest indication of the differences between the earliest forms of Koto; but with regard to the three now in use they can be pointed out with more precision. The Sō-no-koto has low bridges, the strings are coarser and more loosely twisted than those now used, and the *tsumé* are of thick paper, gilt or silvered, with a very small piece of bamboo let in, not more than one-fifth of an inch in length. In playing, the paper stall first rubs the string, the bamboo striking it afterwards, but with very little force; the result is a soft woolly tone. In the Japanese Koto these three points are altered; the bridges are raised, the strings are of finer quality, and the *tsumé* are of ivory standing clear of the leather stall, enabling the strings to be struck clean. The result is a clear bright tone, tending naturally to the production of lighter and brighter music.

The Ikuta-koto is used now almost exclusively in the west of Japan, though occasionally in the east by ladies. Its sides and extremities are

F. H. YAMADA KOTO

THE YAMATO KOTO

covered with elaborate lacquer designs and inlay of tortoise-shell, ivory, and silver; the strings are of different colours, like those of the Western Harp, enabling them to be more easily distinguished and remembered. The *tsumé* are of thick ivory or tortoise-shell set in lacquered leather stalls, and are cut square at the top. In the Yamada-koto, used by all the profession in the east of Japan, superfluous ornament is discarded, the whole art of the maker being devoted to the preparation of the finest wood for the body; only on very costly instruments is a little gold lacquer ornament of the most severe kind introduced. The bridges have again been raised; they are made much stouter, and are either tipped with ivory or made of solid ivory; the strings are of the finest white or yellow silk. The *tsumé* are about an inch long, of ivory in leather stalls, with an elliptical top. On the whole the instrument is more substantial and more workmanlike than the delicately-built Ikuta-koto, and gives a much clearer and more resonant tone.

The three forms of *tsumé* are figured on the plate facing page 144, drawn to their exact sizes.

We have now to go back to the old Koto of Japan, the Yamato-koto—otherwise called *Wa-gon*—which differs essentially in structure and principle from those which have been described. The Japanese authorities agree, and I see neither reason nor authority for disputing with them, in claiming it, as the name indicates, as a purely national instrument. The story of its development from six long bows tied side by side is a familiar one; and the form of the instrument suggests that it is by no means improbable.

The sounding-board of the Yamato-koto is cut at one end into five long notches, the six strings being attached to the six "bow" projections by thick coarse cords. The bridges are made of untrimmed joints of maple twigs; the strings themselves being of coarse twisted silk. The idea of the roughness of the instrument is further preserved in the rule that it ought not to have a case of any sort. Crude though its construction is, its tone is very sweet and mellow.

Again, the principle of the instrument is entirely different from that of the ordinary Koto. The six strings are tuned in the following order—D, F, A, C, E, G,—

the major triad of the tonic, and the minor triad of the second of the
diatonic scale of C major : an interesting and harmonious tonal relation
with which Western musicians are perfectly familiar.

The method of playing is as follows. In the right hand a small slip
of ox-horn, or other hard material, is held, with which all the six strings
are scratched (literally *koto-saki*) rapidly, from the first to the sixth, close to
the long bridge at the right end of the instrument. The strings are then
at once damped with the left hand, and a little melody accompanying the
voice is tinkled out with the eft little finger, the "scratch" coming to
mark the pauses in the rhythm.

The instrument is now used only on the rare occasions when the music
which was originally written for it is performed : the *Kagura*, the *Saibara*,
and the rest of the old music of the country.

The following diagrams of the proper positions of the hand in playing
the Koto are taken from Abé Suyenao's "Records of Ancient Music."

POSITIONS OF THE HANDS IN PLAYING THE *YAMATO-KOTO*.

POSITIONS OF RIGHT HAND HOLDING THE PLECTRUM :—

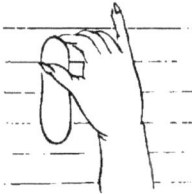

Scratching outwards.

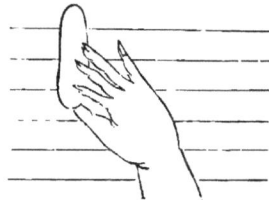

Scratching inwards.

POSITIONS OF LEFT HAND :—

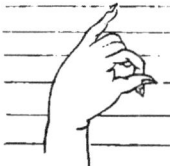

The little finger playing the melody.

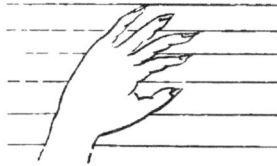

Damping the strings after scratching.

POSITIONS OF THE HANDS IN PLAYING THE *SŌ-NO-KOTO.*

RIGHT-HAND POSITIONS :—

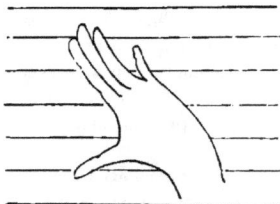

Suga-kaki: thumb striking the string, fingers playing *kaki.*

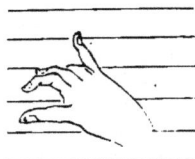

Kō-tsumé: up-stroke of the thumb.

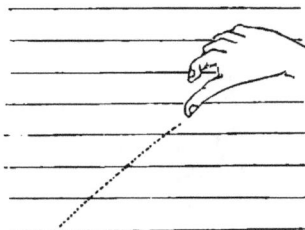

Ren: position of thumb after a sweep over several strings.

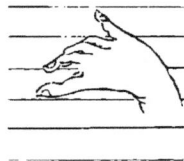

Kacchi-zumé: thumb-stroke.

LEFT-HAND POSITIONS :—

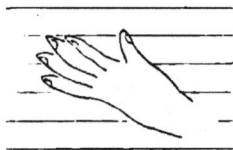

The hand at rest below the bridges.

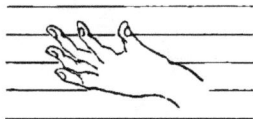

Pressing the string to produce a sharp.

PRINCIPAL MEASUREMENTS OF THE FOUR KOTOS NOW IN USE.

	Yamato-koto. (Old Japanese.)	Sō-no-koto. (Chinese.)	Ikuta-koto.	Yamada-koto.
			(Modern Japanese.)	
Length	6 feet 3 in.	6 feet 4½ in.	6 feet 3 in.	6 feet
Breadth	5¾ in. [upper end] 9¼ in. [lower end]	10 in. 9½ in.	9¾ in.	9½ in.
Depth of sounding board	2 in.	1¾ in.	3 in.	3 in.
Height of upper end	4¼ in.	4½ in.	5 in.	5¼ in.
Height of lower end	3 in.	3½ in.	2½ in.	3½ in.
Height of string bridges	2½ in.	2 in.	2 in.	2¼ in.
Upper bridge from end	3 in.	4½ in.	5¼ in.	4½ in.
Lower bridge from end		10 in.	9½ in.	8 in.
Length of fastening ropes	11½ in.			
Strings apart ...	½ in. at upper bridge 1½ in. at rope fastening Notches of the "bows" project 2¾ inches from lower end	¾ in.	¾ in.	¾ in.

VARIETIES OF THE KIN, OR KOTO.

We have not sufficient information available to attempt a systematic classification of the numerous instruments which fall properly under the head of Kins, or Kotos. The order in which the following instruments are described is based on the preceding account, and is a possible approximation to their order of development.

ICHI-GEN-KIN—the "One-stringed Kin"—or SUMA-KOTO : a one-stringed instrument, said to have been invented in Japan in the Engi era, A.D. 901, at Suma, near Kobé, whence it took its name.

It is made of *kiri* wood, very slightly convexed, and measures 3 feet 7 inches long, by 4½ inches broad. Its one string, 2 feet 9½ inches in length, is fastened underneath the body of the instrument; coming through a small hole at one end, it passes over a low movable bridge and is wound round a peg 4½ inches high, which stands at right-angles to the body at the other end. The string is tuned to F♯, the second string of the Koto, and fundamental note of the scale.

The method of playing is peculiar. Between the thumb and first finger of the right hand is held an ivory *tsumé*, composed of a section of a cylinder, the two ends of which are cut at a right-angle to one another, as shown on Plate XI., page 144. With this the string is struck near the bridge, the stroke being generally upwards ; a down stroke is, however, occasionally introduced in order to obtain variety of intonation. On the second finger of the left hand is worn a heavy ivory cylinder, 2½ inches long, figured on the same Plate. The different notes are produced by resting this cylinder lightly on different parts of the string, the divisions into tones and semitones being indicated by small ivory or painted spots on the face of the body. A peculiar jangling trill is produced by sliding the cylinder along the string to the different positions, instead of lifting it clear.

The one-stringed Koto is said to have been invented by an exiled nobleman to chase away his melancholy ; his original instrument being a string stretched across his hat. There is no doubt, however, that a one-stringed instrument existed in China in very early times. The chroniclers assert that its departed spirit took the usual means of returning to earth, revealing itself in a dream to the exile of Suma.

NI-GEN-KIN — the "Two-stringed Kin": a variety of the Suma-koto, with two strings tuned in unison to F♯. The dimensions of the body are the same, but instead of being flat it is hollowed to a depth of two inches. The strings, fastened underneath as in the Suma-Koto, pass over a bridge with two notches, half-an-inch apart at one end, but instead of going direct to the tuning-pegs, they are brought together on a second bridge with one notch only: thence they pass through a small piece of brass to their respective pegs, which are 2½ inches long. The Ni-gen-kin is played with the same heavy cylindrical *tsumé* as the Suma-koto, the double string emphasizing the trills produced on that instrument. Small pieces of metal are inserted in the body to indicate the positions of the notes.[14]

The Ichi-gen-kin and the Ni-gen-kin are figured on Plate XI., page 144; the one-stringed instrument rests on a low table which is generally used when any of these small Kotos are played.

A variety of the Ni-gen-kin is made of a section of bamboo; the strings are tied to thick silk cords at one end, and pass to the tuning-pegs through a large hole at the other end ; the pegs are placed one on each side of the body. A second hole at the upper end allows the strings to be struck freely. The cords are of purple silk, adorned with heavy tassels.

YAKUMO-KOTO — the "Eight-cloud Koto": a two-stringed instrument, almost identical with the Ni-gen-kin, except that the body is enclosed, thus making a true sounding-board.

SAN-GEN-KIN—the "Three-stringed Kin": a further development of the Suma-koto, with three strings, the outer tuned in unison to C♯, the middle one to F♯, thus :—

giving the first, second, and fifth strings of the Koto. The dimensions of the sounding-board—which is enclosed, as in the case of the Yakumo-koto —are the same as those of the one and two-stringed instruments; and the same heavy *tsumé* and cylinder are used by the player.

CYLINDRICAL TSUMÉ FOR THE ICHI-GEN-KIN   FOR THE SŌ-NO-KOTO   FOR THE YAMADA-KOTO   FOR THE IKUTA-KOTO

The third string, C♯, is used for the melody, the first and second for the *kaké* beat. The melody, moreover, is occasionally reinforced by the F♯ of the second string, whole passages being played in fifths. The three strings are also often struck together in quick *arpeggio* fashion.

As in the case of the Ni-gen-kin, a variety of the San-gen-kin is sometimes made of a segment of bamboo. It is a simple reproduction, however, of the original, without the silk cords and tassels, and without the apertures in the body. The pegs are disposed at right-angles to one another, two at the sides and one in the centre of the body.

AZUMA-KOTO — the "Eastern Koto": another three-stringed instrument with a perfect sounding-board. Certain differences in its structure are, however, very important to notice. Three wires are strung loosely inside, which produce slight vibrations when the instrument is played. These wires do not rattle like the one which is fixed inside the Gekkin, but seem to be used for sympathetic vibrations, like those of the Viol d'Amore, though they are not tuned to special notes as are those of the more modern Western instrument.

The upper end of the sounding-board is cut into three bow-notches, showing the affinity between this Koto and the Yamato-koto; it is also bound thrice in its length with wicker, to preserve the idea of three bows being tied together. Purple silk tassels hang from two small holes in the side.

In the next group the instruments are constructed on somewhat different principles, and are played in a different way. Instead of the loose bridges which are used in the one, two, and three-stringed Kotos, one long fixed bridge is placed at each end; the tuning-pegs have disappeared, and the strings passing under the sounding-board are tuned permanently, and not as occasion requires; and, finally, the cylindrical *tsumé* are not used, the strings being plucked with the thumb and first finger. The strings are stopped with the fingers of the left hand, the positions of the notes being indicated, as in the first group, by marks on the sounding-board.*

* I have to regret that my information on this group of Kotos is exceedingly meagre, and I have some doubt whether it is altogether reliable. The instruments are seldom used, and there are few people who possess any knowledge of them. I have occasionally supplemented my own observations by those of Monsieur Alexandre Kraus Fils, published in his pamphlet, "La Musique du Japon," which he permits me to refer to.

U

It will be easily understood, however, that there are links connecting the two groups, in which some of the characteristics of both are noticeable : these links are the five and the six-stringed Kotos. The resemblances to the first group seem to show that the natural order of development is as I have given them, although the absence of *tsumé* and the more primitive method of playing point to the second group as the earlier.

Go-kin—the "Five-stringed Kin." The body is the same length as that of the Suma-koto, and only slightly broader. It is in the same way slightly convexed, and has the two lateral indentations which are shown in the figure of the Suma-koto facing page 144 ; the lower bridge is movable.

"Le Gokkine rappelle son origine Chinoise par ses deux enfoncements latéraux. Il est monté de cinq cordes dont les trois plus grosses sont jaunes ; la quatrième est violette, et la cinquième, bleue. Au lieu des points blancs du Souma-koto, il y a sur le Gokkine, en charactères Chinois, les noms des sons que l'on produit, en appuyant sur la corde aux endroits marqués. On tourne les chevilles à l'aide d'une clef à bois."—[*Kraus.*]

Roku-kin — the "Six-stringed Kin": an instrument with six strings passing over two fixed bridges, one at each end of the sounding-board. The sides of the body are parallel, and the characteristic lateral indentations are wanting.

Shichi-gen-kin — the "Seven-stringed Kin." This is the most important instrument of the group now under consideration, and it is greatly to be regretted that information respecting it is so very meagre. The accompanying illustration shows the front and the back of the instrument.

The length of the sounding-board is 3 feet 10½ inches, with a string length of 3 feet 7 inches. The breadth, 6½ inches, tapering to 4¼ ; the height at the upper end 3½ inches, at the lower end 1¾ : the thickness, 1 inch at the outside edges, and 1¾ inch at the centre of the convexity.

The strings are tied to loops of silk cord, which are fastened underneath the sounding-board to seven small pegs ; the cords come up to the upper surface through small holes, the knots between the cords and the strings resting on a bridge, half an inch high, which serves to keep the strings free of the sounding-board. On the bridge the strings are three-quarters of an inch apart; from this point they converge, and passing over the lower end, which is slightly raised to form a bridge, within a space of an inch and a quarter, they are tightly wound round two stout pegs fastened underneath

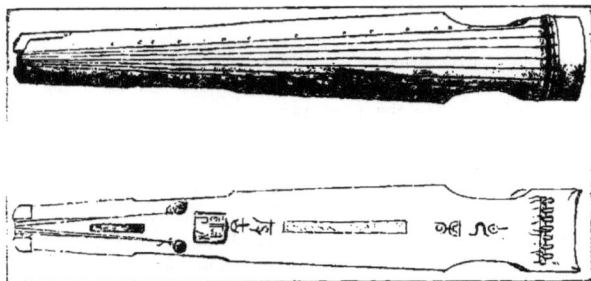

FRONT AND BACK VIEW OF THE SHICHI-GEN-KIN.

the sounding-board one foot from the end; these pegs serve as rests for the instrument. It will be observed from this description that the strings of the Shichi-gen-kin can only be tuned by untying the knots at their upper ends.

The body has the characteristic lateral indentations : and the positions for the stopping are indicated by small ivory circles.

The tuning of the strings is remarkable :—

or, raising the notes to the Koto pitch :—

A, E, G, F♯, G, E, F♯.

The method of playing is, however, more remarkable still. The melody is played entirely by "plucking" the last string, the first and second fingers of the left hand being used for stopping. The remaining strings are swept in *arpeggio* by the thumb of the right hand.

Monsieur Kraus calls this instrument the Chinese Kin.

The Kin, however, was undoubtedly, like all the Chinese instruments of the class, a much larger instrument. It may possibly be the miniature Kin, in vogue in China during the Chin dynasty, its length corresponding with the length of that instrument as given in the *Encyclopædia*. If this supposition should be correct, it furnishes us with the important conclusion that the development of the Hitsu-no-koto from the Kin, or, as it is sometimes called, the Kin-no-koto, was accomplished by means of the addition of a movable bridge or fret for each string. Monsieur Kraus, however, gives both the Shichi-gen-kin, and its companion the Gindai, with movable bridges. The presence of the "stopping-points" on the sounding-board seems to show, however, that this is inaccurate.

GINDAI : an instrument of precisely the same size and shape as the preceding, but strung with thirteen strings.—[*Kraus.*] The name is probably made out of the words "*dai kin*"—*i.e.*, the "larger Kin."

KAKU-GOTO — the "Square Koto"; "un autre instrument Japonais de la plus haute antiquité, tombé aujourd'hui en désuétude." It is rectangular, being 2 feet long by 1 foot 6 inches broad, with a string-length of 1 foot 5 inches. There are twenty-five strings, stretched over two long fixed bridges ; it is played with hard wooden *tsumé.*—[*Kraus.*]

SAGE-KOTO : a small Koto of very ancient origin, said to have been invented in the year 3468 B.C. It has nine strings, and measures 2 feet long, with a string-length of 1 foot 6 inches : its breadth at the upper end is 6 inches, and at the lower end 4¾ inches.

The group diverges at this point in two directions : the Nichin, forming a connecting link between the Koto and the Gekkin ; and the Tsuma-koto, which seems to show traces of foreign influence.

NICHIN : a circular Koto, with a diameter of 1 foot 3 inches, and a string-length of 1 foot. The thickness of the body is 2 inches.

" Le Nichine est une espèce de psaltérion rond, sur lequel sont tendues six cordes de grosseur et de couleurs différentes. La première, beaucoup plus grosse que les autres, est jaune et donne l'octave basse de la tonique ; la seconde est bleu clair, la cinquième, noire, et la sixième, blanche. Ces six cordes sont attachées à un bouton en bois et passent au dessus de deux chevalets placés à o^m.32, l'un de l'autre ; on les accorde en tournant leurs chevilles avec une petite clef en bois. Il est pourvu à l'intérieur d'une petite lame en fer, qui se trouve dans la plupart des instruments populaires au Japon et qui sert à faire un petit bruit, quand on remue l'instrument."—[*Kraus.*]

The circular shape and the vibrating wire seem to show clearly the process by which the Gekkin was developed from the Koto.

TSUMA-KOTO : a Koto with thirteen strings on a sounding-board in the form of a trapezoid. Its measurements are as follows :—Greatest length, 2 feet 2 inches ; shortest length, 1 foot 7 inches ; breadth, 11 inches. Each string is attached to a small tuning-peg on the upper surface, resembling those used in the Piano.—[*Kraus.*] Monsieur Kraus gives to this instrument movable bridges for each string. I am inclined to doubt whether this information is accurate, as the presence of tuning-pegs seems to indicate that bridges would not be used.

YA-GOTO—the "Eight-stringed Koto": an instrument said to have been developed out of the Yamato-koto. Its distinguishing feature is that it is double-strung. The sounding-board measures 3 feet 7 inches long by about 5 inches high, and is more convexed than that of any other Koto. The eight double strings pass over two long low bridges, giving a string length of 32 inches. Above the upper bridge they pass through ivory holes let into the surface of the sounding-board, and are wound round eight long tuning-pegs which are fastened underneath. These pegs terminate in small spear-heads, which project from the upper end of the instrument.

YAN-KIN : the Chinese form of the Zither, the shape of which is accurately copied. It is strung with fifteen double wires, and is said by the instrument makers to have come to China from Italy.

Another double-stringed instrument, sometimes called the Yo-KIN, with thirteen double brass wires, has probably developed out of this adaptation of the Zither, though it is said to be of Japanese origin. The sounding-board is of black wood, measuring 26 inches by 10 ; it is 4 inches high, convexed, and decorated with metal ornaments. The wires are attached to a double row of tuning-pegs placed at both ends beyond the bridges.

In the last group the instruments are distinguished by the introduction of the small movable bridges for each string, which have already been noticed.

In this group come two instruments which have already been mentioned, but of which no accurate description can be given :—

HITSU-NO-KOTO : an instrument of which there were many varieties, the largest having fifty strings.

CHIKU-NO-KOTO : a thirteen-stringed instrument, struck with a short bamboo.

There are also the following, which have already been described :—

YAMATO-KOTO : the old six-stringed Koto of Japan.

SO-NO-KOTO : the ultimate form of the thirteen-stringed Kin of China.

IKUTA-KOTO and YAMADA-KOTO : the ultimate forms of the thirteen-stringed Koto of Japan.

To these must be added :—

HAN-KOTO—the "Half-Koto" : the ordinary Japanese Koto in miniature, which is used on journeys.

YŌ-KIN—the "Chinese Koto" : a miniature thirteen-stringed instrument from China. Its measurements are as follows :— Length, 3 feet 7 inches ; breadth, 9 inches ; height at the sides, 5 inches.

THE YŌ-KIN.

Two forms of Corean Kotos must be mentioned here which are given in the *Encyclopædia*. The drawings show one to have been somewhat in the ordinary form, with a figure-head at one end—the Kudara-koto, or Corean Koto ; the other—the Shiragi-koto—seems to have resembled the traditional form of the ancient Harp.

Although the amount of information at present procurable is not all that could be desired, there is sufficient to indicate how important a position the Koto holds in the development of stringed instruments of music. All authorities are, I think, agreed that the long-bow of the archers first suggested the tight-drawn string as a sound-producing body. Development seems to have been along two distinct lines. There is first the well-known one, the multiplication of strings on the same bow, one behind the other,

OLD COREAN KOTOS.

which speedily produced the early forms of Harp : and it is somewhat curious to note that the Shiragi-koto of Corea is the only trace of this form in the three Kingdoms of the Far East.

Secondly, there is the multiplication of bows as well as strings, the weapons being placed side by side and tied together. The Koto family springs immediately from this idea, and it seems probable that the sounding-board sprang from this class rather than from an amplification of the arc of the bow.*

---

* In considering the bow-theory of the development of the Koto, it is impossible not to refer to the Valiha, a remarkable instrument in use in Madagascar. This instrument is of the Koto family. It is made of a piece of entire bamboo ; the strings are made of thin slices of the reed, raised on bridges, but unsevered from the main stem which forms the sounding-board. The strings completely encircle the bamboo, the instrument being played upright.

Finally, the archery bow reappears in the bow of the Fiddle class as the vibrator instead of the vibrating instrument.

The subordinate points of development are also to be noticed.

The body of the instrument appears first as a flat piece of wood very slightly convexed, then as a fully-curved hollow resonator, and lastly, as a regular enclosed sounding-board.

At a certain stage loose vibrating wires are introduced into the sounding-board, which afterwards give place to a noisy jangling wire.

The strings, at first arranged unmethodically, and of any number from one to fifty, afterwards settle down to thirteen, capable of producing the thirteen notes in the octave. Double strings are, after a time, introduced, and become the regular features in a certain class of instruments. Much later, wire is introduced, instead of string soaked in wax; but this never seems to have become popular.

The strings are, in the early instruments, attached to large tuning-pegs; these diminish in size till they become small pins turned with a key instead of by hand. Where the movable bridges are introduced the pegs or pins are discarded altogether, the strings being fastened either below or above the sounding-board.

The strings are vibrated either by the finger or with a plectrum, which at first is a small piece of horn, and afterwards developes into the large *bachi* of the Biwa and Samisen; and then dwindles again into the Koto *tsumé*, worn on the thumb and first and second fingers.

This continued process of development will be traced further in the two remaining classes of stringed instruments: those with frets—the Biwas; and those without frets—the Samisens and Fiddles.

We may proceed now to consider certain points of interest in connection with the Koto notation and the method of playing that instrument.

TECHNICAL TERMS USED FOR KOTO MUSIC.

Ritsu—a semitone.

THE SHARPS.

Osu—to press: *i.e.* to press a string below its bridge and thus sharpen its tone. The pressure should raise the natural note of the string one *ritsu*; the term is therefore equivalent to the Western "sharp." It is commonly called *ka*, the Japanese sign being 刀. Thus, *ku osu*, or *ku ka*, means the ninth string pressed, and it may be properly translated by A♯.[19]

There are, in addition, three other varieties of sharps.

É, the "after sharp": the pressure being applied below the bridge *after* the string has been struck. The pressure is retained until the next note is played. The Japanese sign is 工, and it might be conveniently rendered for purposes of translation by the sign ♯. *Ku é*, or 9 ♯, would be interpreted on the Western staff thus:—

Ké—the "twisted sharp": sharp vibrations are introduced into the natural ones of the string by twisting it slightly below its bridge with the thumb and first finger, the natural vibrations being then allowed to continue. The Japanese sign is ♭, and it may be conveniently rendered by ♯. *Ku ké*, or 9 ♯, would be interpreted thus on the staff:—

Yū—the "half sharp": sharp vibrations are, as in *ké*, introduced into the natural ones of the string by a pressure below the string: but the pressure is removed before the next note is played.[20] The higher vibrations therefore predominate, but the relapse into the natural is allowed to be distinctly heard, unless it occurs in a quick passage. The Japanese sign is 工, and it may be conveniently rendered by ♯. *Ku yū*, or 9 ♯, would be interpreted as nearly as possible on the staff by—

Nijū oshi—the double pressure, which raises the natural note of the string a full tone. The proper use of the double-pressure is, according to Mr. Yamasé's explanation, to produce the notes of the scale which are not given by the open strings. Thus, the phrase in "*Kasuga-mōde*,"

> 9
> 10
> *to ka*
> *to nijū oshi*

translated on to the Western staff, becomes—

There is not an unnatural temptation to call this a "double sharp," but the refinements of the double sharp, as distinguished from the note which represents it on the Piano, are, I think, unknown to the Japanese musician. In translating on to the Western staff, it may be necessary occasionally to use the double sharp, as in the inverted *kaki* given below, but this would occur in Japanese music more frequently with a simple than with a double pressure.

Examples of *ka*, *é*, *ké*, and *yū*, will be found in the specimen of Koto notation given on page 162, the translation of which on to the Western staff will be found on page 116.

Agari—to raise a string from its normal tuning one semitone or more, by moving its bridge up.

Sagari—to lower a string a semitone or more, by moving its bridge down. One of the tunings is called *Go-sagari roku-agari*, in consequence of such changes in the fifth and sixth strings.

There is obviously no other way of flattening the natural note of a string: where a flattening is required, therefore, the bridge is moved by the left hand during the progress of the piece. This occurs to the 6th and *to* strings during the progress of the tune "*Kurama-jishi*," written in *Hirajōshi* with those strings raised a semitone—Tuning No. 11, on the scheme of Koto-tunings given on page 92.

Kaki—"to scratch": two adjoining strings struck in succession with the same finger, sometimes quickly, sometimes slowly : thus *kaki* on the first and second would be :—

and on the fifth and sixth it would be :—

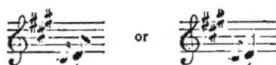

It is often used to mark a pause in the melody, as in "*Saita-Sakurai*"; and in the same way to mark the conclusion of a part of the composition, or as we might say "variation," as in "*Rokudan*." In this case the *kaki* is always on the first and second strings, and is played more vigorously, like a short roll on a drum, a strong accent being laid on the second note.[21]

In the Japanese notation the strings on which *kaki* is to be played are only indicated by being written close together : but, as ordinary quavers are written in the same way, the *kaki*, like so many other things, has to be remembered by the player. The following would be a convenient method of indicating *kaki* in turning Japanese notation into English figures :—

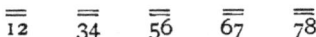

$$\overline{\overline{12}} \quad \overline{\overline{34}} \quad \overline{\overline{56}} \quad \overline{\overline{67}} \quad \overline{\overline{78}}$$

These five are in commonest use : they are played with the first or second finger.

Haya-kaki—"quick or double *kaki*:" two *kaki* beats played in quick succession ; *haya-kaki* on the sixth and seventh strings, for example, would be written thus :—

Warizumé—an inverted *kaki* on the eighth and seventh strings, with a "half sharp" (*yū*) on the seventh : it is played slowly, and is often used in the concluding phrase of a composition, the *yū* being prolonged ; it may be thus rendered on the staff :—

Another inverted *kaki* is sometimes found on the thirteenth and twelfth strings, the latter sharpened ; it has, however, no distinct name, being written simply *kin, i ka :* on the staff this is :—

Hazamu—a short phrase in frequent use, composed of the tenth string dotted, followed by the ninth and eighth : translated on to the staff thus :—

Kaké—the name given to a phrase of five notes of frequent occurrence : it may be given on any string, the number of the string on which it ends being written before the word *kaké ;* the phrase consists of two consecutive strings played with the first finger ; then two, one string lower, played with the second ; then one with the thumb, four strings higher ; thus :—

to kaké   7   8   6   7   *to*

i kaké   8   9   7   8   *i*

kin kaké   9   10 8   9   *kin*

jū kaké   6   7   5   6   10

hachi kaké   4   5   3   4   8

roku kaké   2   3   1   2   6

and so on.

The piece "*Umegae*" is built up on this phrase. An interesting variation of it occurs, in which the *kaké* is shorn of its last two notes : thus *shichi kaké*, 3, 4, 2, 3, 7, appears as 3, 4, 2 :—

In the example of notation it will be seen that, although the numbers of the strings composing the *kaké* are written in their proper sequence, the name is written at the side to enable the performer to phrase the notes properly.

Kaké is literally "to superpose," referring to the thumb note which stands up prominently above the gentle swaying of the first four notes of the phrase ; and with the exception of *roku kaké*, this superposed note is the octave of the third note.

So far as I have been able to observe no common phrases, with the exception of *kaké* and *hazumu*, have special names given to them.

GLISSADES.

Nagashi, or *omoté*—"to flow" : a slide or *glissando* with the first finger over the strings ; both the first and last strings of the slide are named ; *nagashi* is, however, generally used for the common glissade 1 to *kin*.[22]

Hikiren is used for shorter glissades from the first string, as from 1 to 6, 1 to 10.

In rapid movements *hikiren* is often only a swift sweep over the strings from right to left of the first and second fingers held together, without much regard to the actual strings struck.

Uraren is also used for short glissades—those starting downwards from the last string. This is a very graceful *glissade*, often used in finishing part of a composition ; it is played with the first and second fingers turned back, moving slowly with a slight circular motion outwards, finishing with an inverted *kaki* on the indicated string played with the thumb.

Thus *roku-madé uraren* is a slide from *kin* to 6, or *kin* to 7̄6̄.

Namigaeshi—"waves coming and going" : probably in allusion to the fanciful idea of a dragon lying on the sea-shore which the form of the Koto suggests. *Namigaeshi* is made up of alternate glissades over all the strings, from 1 to *kin*, and back from *kin* to 1 ; this is done once or twice, and occasionally thrice, in all cases terminating with an upward *nagashi*, or with a *hikiren* from 1 to $\bar{5}6$:—

First Namigaeshi.

Second Namigaeshi.

Nagashi.

or, for the last bar, *Hikiren*, 1 to $\bar{5}6$—

Shū—"to whistle": a moderately rapid sweep with the edge of the *tsumé* from right to left on one string, generally the sixth ; the first and second fingers are held closely together : it must be cleanly finished.

Surizumé—"rubbing with the fingers": a double sweep from right to left and back from left to right, also on one string, which is held tightly between the *tsumé* of the first and second fingers. *Surizumé*, like *shū*, is moderately rapid, must be cleanly finished, and is usually confined to the sixth string.

Awaseru—"to put together": hence, "to harmonize."

It is used both for octaves as well as other harmonies, the commonest examples of which are the following. "Harmonies" may be indicated thus in English :—

$${}^{8}_{3}]\quad {}^{9}_{5}]\quad {}^{7}_{2}]\quad {}^{to}_{8}$$

the Japanese sign is 合.

In octaves the upper note is called *kan*, the lower *ryô*. *Awaseru* is also used for the unison of the first and fifth strings, which is frequently met with.

$$\frac{5}{1}]$$

Haneru—an up-stroke with the first or second finger, the edge, instead of the face of the *tsumé*, striking the string.

Sukui—an up-stroke with the thumb, commonly used to finish a sequence of rapid beats either on the same or a lower string.

A down and an up-stroke with the thumb on the same string are often used in rapid succession; no special name is given to this. The edge of the *tsumé* is used in this case for both notes.

Both the up and the up-and-down strokes have corresponding phrases on the Samisen; when the latter occurs on the Koto, a trill is played on the Samisen by touching the string lightly with the third or fourth finger, above the finger which presses the note, directly after the string is struck with the *bachi*. The following are examples from "*Kasuga-môde*," rendered on the staff :—

Example of *Sukui :* the four semiquavers are played with rapid down-beats of the thumb, the quaver following with the up-stroke of the thumb.

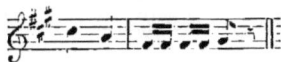

Example of *Sukui :* the second of each group of semiquavers is played with an up-stroke of the thumb, the first with a down-stroke, the edge of the *tsumé* being used for both.

Example of *Sukui* and *Haneru :* the groups of semiquavers are played as in the last example, the succeeding quavers with an up-stroke of the first and second fingers alternately.

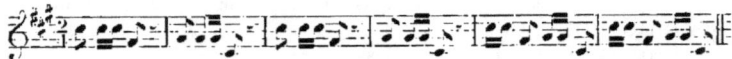

The same phrase as rendered on the *Samisen :* the middle note of each triplet is produced by the light pressure of the finger on the string, the succeeding quaver is sounded by the open string being plucked by a finger of the left hand near the neck.

Although triplets accurately represent the Samisen phrase, they would alter the character of the phrase on the Koto; the accent, however, is on the first note of each of the "doublets," in the same way as the accent falls on the first note of a triplet.

Maoteru—" to measure the interval "; a rest or pause.[24]

Uchi—beating with the left hand on the strings below the bridges, during long pauses : it is used whether the song is continued during the pause or not.

The word *hayaku* is sometimes used as we use *accelerando*. Where the notes are of less value than the common unit of time, which I have taken as a crotchet of ¾ time—a passage of quavers for example—the numbers of the strings are written close together, in a manner now to be explained.

In the following diagrams are given, on the left, a specimen of the notation used for Koto music ; on the right, an English rendering of it. It is half of the first verse of "*Umegae*." [23]

The columns are to be read downwards and from right to left. Each column is divided into four : on the left are the words of the song (omitted in the English translation) ; then follow three kinds of circles ; the numbers of the strings come next ; and lastly, the directions as to phrasing and accidentals.

The circles require to be explained first : they are the marks for the bars. The large circles, of which there are two kinds, to prevent the eye getting confused, mark the commencement of the bars ; the small circles mark the half-bars. Taking the time as ¾, the distance between the large and small circles represents one crotchet ; the number of the string to be played is printed opposite the circle. Quavers and semiquavers are indicated by the position which the numbers of the strings occupy in the intervening space ; thus, if there are two quavers on the first beat of the bar, and a crotchet on the second, the first quaver would stand opposite the large circle, the crotchet opposite the small circle, and the second quaver halfway between the two. Similarly. if there is a dotted quaver followed by a semiquaver and then a crotchet, the quaver stands opposite the circle belonging to the beat, the semiquaver close to the crotchet which is opposite to the next circle. The rests are marked in precisely the same way, the position of the succeeding string indicating the duration of the rest.

It will be observed that *kandō*—the commencement—is also marked by a small circle, and that the half-bars belonging to the bars at the bottom of the columns run over on to the next. I have not found any satisfactory explanation of this. I believe, however, that pieces generally begin with a beat of the left hand, and that this is indicated by the first small circle.

The numbers of the strings are put, as I have said, by the side of the circles, but it will be seen that some of the numbers are more to the right than others. Where the figures are in their normal position the thumb is to be used; where they stand nearer the circles the first finger is to be used; where they stand away to the right the second finger is to be used.

The little dash which occasionally follows the number of the string indicates that the note is to be repeated. Occasionally two or more dashes will be found occurring in their proper relative positions between the circles.

The different marks for the sharps, which are placed after the string numbers, have already been explained.

This form of notation is, I believe, common in the East. When it is understood it is amply sufficient for all purposes; and in the translated form, as I have given it, I find everything that is needful for playing the instrument. For the stringed instruments without frets I have not been able to discover any form of notation, though I believe it does exist. For the stringed instruments with frets, and for the Flutes, Hichiriki and Shō, a notation on a principle identical with that of the Koto exists, the number of the fret to be pressed, or of the hole to be stopped, being indicated.*

---

* The Rev. Marmaduke E. Browne informs me that the notation for the Salvation Army Concertina is based on this principle, the melodies being written with numbers indicating which buttons are to be pressed, and with extra marks where the thumb goes, and where to push in and pull out.

FAC-SIMILE OF A PAGE OF KOTO MUSIC.

ORIGINAL.

[The first two lines on page 116 render this page of music on staff notation.]

Umegae.

No. 1

Printed according to

the Original Copy.

				Kandō—the commencement.
— 9̄ 10 *ka*	— 10	— 10		
— 8 *i kaké*	— 7 *to kaké*	— 8 *i kaké*	— 7 *to kaké*	
— 9	— 8	— 9	— 8	
═ 7	═ 6	═ 7	═ 6	
— 8	— 7	— 8	— 7	
i ✠ *é*	— *to*	*i* ✠ *é*	— *to*	
— Γ *uchi*	— 10	— *uchi*	— *uchi*	
═ *to*	═ *to i* ✠ *é*	═ *to*	═ *i* ✠ *é*	
— 10	— *uchi*	— 10	— *to*	
i ✠ *é*	— 8 *kin*] *awaseru*	*i* ✠ *é*	— 10	
— *uchi*	— *uchi*	— *uchi*	— *uchi* 5	
══ 6 6	═ 1̄2̄ *kaki*	═ 6 6	═ *i* ✠ *é* 5	
— *to* ✠ *yu*	— *kin*	— *to* ✠ *yu*	— *to*	
to ✠ *yu*		*to* ✠ *yu*		
⊐ *i* ✠ *uchi ké*	— *kin* ✠ *ka*	⊐ *i* ✠ *uchi ké*	*i* ✠ *ké* 10	
to ✠ *yu* 10	— *i* ✠ *uchi ké*	*to* ✠ *yu* 10	— *uchi* 5 5	
	to ✠ *yu*			
═ 9̄ *ka*	═ 10	═ 9̄ *ka*	═ 9̄ *ka* 5	

BIWAS, AND STRINGED INSTRUMENTS WITH FRETS.

THE position which the Biwa holds in the history of musical development in Japan has already been explained. It was brought from China by the commissioners sent to that country by the Emperor Jimmyō, about the year 935 A.D. It is attributed by the Chinese to "the Barbarians," and was probably a development from some instruments in use in other Oriental countries, but from which it is difficult to say. Its position in what may be called the "natura order" of musical instruments seems fairly clear: it stands at the head of the second great group of stringed instruments, as the Sō-no-koto stands at the head of the first group. As in the case of the Sō-no-koto, modifications rather than material alterations, were introduced by the Japanese, so in the case of the Biwa, similar modifications were introduced after it had left its home in the Celestial Empire. The modifications were in the direction of lightening and clearing the tone, and making the instrument less unwieldy. But they were still Biwas, and flourished without destroying the vitality of the parent instrument. A national music sprang up, lighter in its nature, more "bird-like" than the ponderous chords which swept from the Chinese strings; but when the old music of China was performed as the accompaniment of the Bugaku dances, the old Biwa was still, and is still, to be found side by side with the old Sō-no-koto, reinforcing its woolly tones with rich and sonorous *arpeggios;* and thence came its modern distinguishing name—the "Bugaku-biwa."

The process by which the Biwa group developed from the Koto group is easily accounted for.

In the Kotos only about one-third of the string-length is used for producing the notes. To gather the strings below the bridges into a narrower compass, and reduce two-thirds of the sounding-board into a neck, must, very early in the history of the instruments, have appeared feasible. To reduce the number of the strings without reducing the compass of the instrument was an easy matter for musicians accustomed to Kotos with one string only. Fixing the loose Koto bridges as frets upon the neck must have followed in due course; Oriental ingenuity finally displaying itself in making the frets of different heights, so that the strings should pass freely over the lower frets to those higher up on the neck. But in the Biwa we find the development thus roughly indicated not in progress, but in its final stage of completeness; the intermediate stages are omitted, and nothing remains to-day to which we can point with certainty as the Biwa in embryo. The Gekkin may have preceded the Biwa, but the dates vouchsafed to us by the books do not afford any reliable guide: the only visible link between the two groups is the circular Koto, the Nichin, which very probably suggested the circular body of the Gekkin. A curious link between the East and the West must here be noted in passing: the upper end of the neck of the Biwa, in which the tuning-pegs are placed, is bent back at right-angles in the same way as the old Theorbo Lyre, which is sometimes seen in mediæval pictures. In the Biwa this serves the purpose of allowing the instrument to rest on the ground while it is being tuned.

The BUGAKU-BIWA is a massive stringed instrument, with a gourd-shaped body measuring 3 feet 3 inches long and 16 inches across the broadest part of the face, and having a string-length of 25 inches. It is said formerly to have been played on horseback. Now it rests on its lower edge on the ground between the knees of the performer, seated, in Japanese fashion, on the floor. It has four strings passing over three high frets and collected in a notch at the upper end. The normal tuning is a combination of *ni-agari* and *san-sagari*. The other tunings will be found in the diagram of the tunings of the Sō-no-koto on page 93, with which it is invariably used for private performances of the Bugaku dances. It is played with a *bachi* of hard wood; but this is very much heavier than that of the Samisen, and has rounded instead of pointed ends. It is grasped firmly in the right hand and dragged over the band of black leather which runs across the face of the instrument, and over the strings, which are strung close to the body, actually striking only the third or fourth string, on which the melody is thus played. The effect of the music, therefore, is that of a series of open chords. The tone of instrument is sonorous and rich.

The body of the Biwa is made of *shitan*, the neck of willow, and tuning-handles of peach: the *bachi* of "yellow willow." The side, like that of the

Koto, is called *ō-iso*—the sea-shore. The measurements are given on page 168, with the corresponding ones of the Satsuma-biwa for convenience of comparison.

It appears that after the Biwa was established in Japan some slight variations were introduced, one, and sometimes two, frets being added. The 5-fret instrument is figured on the opposite page. The instruments with 3, 4, and 5 frets are all in use at the present time.

The SATSUMA-BIWA, figured on the opposite page, is a smaller and more delicate instrument than the Bugaku-biwa, from which it was developed in Kagoshima, where it was afterwards used to accompany the *Heiké-monogatari* recitations.

Four larger frets, rather less than half an inch in breadth, are placed on the neck, but in different positions from those on the Chinese Biwa. The notes are produced by varying pressures above the frets, the strings being struck with a very large *bachi*: a peculiar bird-like trill is imparted to the notes by the vibrations of the string on the broad surface of the fret. These delicate vibrations are emphasized by the up and down stroke with the *bachi*, which is a chief characteristic of the music.[26] Its tones depend for their accuracy both on the position of the fingers between the frets, and also on the amount of pressure placed upon them; the frets stand up from the neck about an inch, and as many as five semitones can be produced by a finger in one position.

The leathern band which runs across the body of the Bugaku-biwa is replaced by a broad band of black ornamented lacquer; the belly is made of polished mulberry or cherry wood, the back and neck being inscribed with poems and the fanciful name of the instrument in bold gold lettering, *e.g.* " Phœnix-voiced!" At the point where the neck meets the back it expands into a large conical form, called *tōyama*—"the distant mountain"; in the face are two ivory crescents—" new moons "—6½ inches from the lowest fret; in each of these a very small aperture is cut. In the Bugaku-biwa the apertures are themselves crescent-shaped, and are rather larger; there is also a circular aperture underneath the string-holder.

The strings are fastened at the base to a large holder, which stands clear of the body except at its lower end: the strings at the holder are one inch apart in both instruments; they get closer together as they pass over

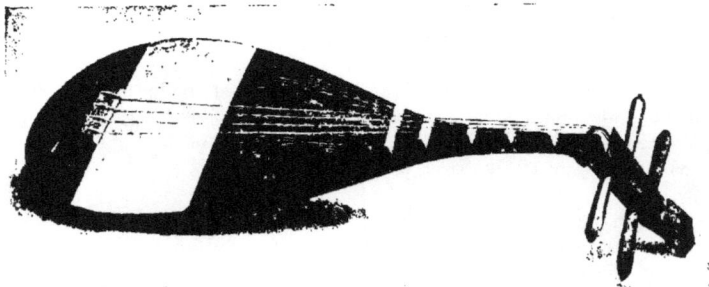

THE FUGAKU-BIWA, WITH 5 FRETS.

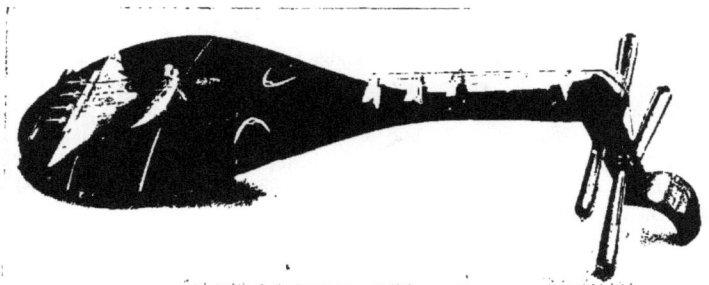

THE SATSUMA-BIWA, WITH LACHE.

THE CHINESE BIWA.

the frets, finally meeting in an ivory or ebony notch at the head of the neck, which comes down at right-angles to the body.

The frets are broad, sloping down to about an inch where they are fastened to the neck, and increase in height from an inch to an inch and a half, thus allowing the strings to pass clear of the lower frets when the pressure is on one higher up.

The strings are tuned to A, E, A. C :—

The first and second are almost invariably used as open strings; the third string is also often used open, very few touched notes being played on it, the melody being left almost entirely to the upper string, which is drawn clear of the others by the little finger of the left hand. Being lighter than the Bugaku-biwa, it is played sitting, with the instrument resting on the right leg. The *répertoire* consists of over one hundred pieces, of which, however, only thirty are considered classical.

The following table shows the comparative measurements of the Bugaku-biwa and the Satsuma-biwa :—

	BUGAKU-BIWA. Chinese.		SATSUMA-BIWA. Japanese.	
	Feet.	Inches.	Feet.	Inches.
Full length .	3	3	3	
Length of neck, measured from lowest fret		8·5	1	1
Breadth of neck . { tapering from		1		1·2
{ to		1·5		1·4
Depth of neck .		1·2		1·3
Length of neck rest, in which the tuning pegs are placed . .		9·5		11
Length of tuning pegs .		4·25		5·5
Greatest breadth of belly	1	4	1	1
Greatest thickness of belly .		2·5		2
Thickness at edge of belly (both faces being slightly convexed) .		1·5		1
Distances of apertures from lowest fret .		11		6·5
Breadth of leather or lacquer band .		7·25		4·8
Length of string-holder at base of belly .		3·5		3·2
Breadth ,, ,, ,,		5·25		4·8
Length of belly below string-holder .		·5		·8
Distance of strings apart at the string-holder .		1		1

	BUGAKU-BIWA. Chinese.		SATSUMA-BIWA. Japanese.	
STRING AND FRET MEASUREMENTS.				
	Feet.	Inches.	Feet.	Inches.
Length of string from the holder to the first fret at the nape of the neck	2	1	1	5·5
Length of string between first and second frets . . .		1		2·1
,, ,, second and third frets . . .		1·1		2
,, ,, third and fourth frets . . .		—		4·8
,, ,, third fret and ivory notch . . .		5·1		—
,, ,, fourth fret and ivory notch . . .		—		1·6
Height of frets — First		·3		1
Second		·35		1·1
Third		·4		1·3
Fourth		—		1·5
Length of frets — First		1		2·5
Second		2		2·5
Third		1		2·5
Fourth		—		1·8
Breadth of frets		·3		·45
BACHI MEASUREMENTS.				
Length		7·5		6·5
Length of striking edge . .		2·75		9·5

The CHINESE BIWA, figured on page 166, is a Chinese modification of the Bugaku-biwa used for lighter music. As the picture shows, it is smaller than the Satsuma-biwa; it has ten frets on the face of the body, and four on the neck. These four upper frets are exceedingly interesting on account of their semi-cylindrical form. They are obviously derived from the heavy cylindrical *tsumé* used in playing the one and two-stringed Kotos, and form one more link between the two families of instruments.

The GEKKIN, sometimes called the " Miniature Biwa," and sometimes the " Moon-shaped Koto," is a Chinese instrument much used in Japan. Although it differs entirely in construction from the Biwa, its high frets clearly show the family likeness. The illustration of " The Gekkin Player" will be found facing page 6.

z

The body is circular, 14 inches in diameter, and 1½ inch thick, the two surfaces being parallel; they are without apertures; on the upper face are generally placed two carved flowers where the apertures would be. The neck is one foot long and 1¼ inch broad, capped by a large flat-headed ornament. There are in all nine frets, decreasing in height, like those of the Biwa: the upper one, over which the strings pass to the pegs, is half an inch in height, and is placed 5½ inches up the neck. Four of the frets are on the face of the instrument, one at the joint of the neck and the body, the remainder on the neck.

There are four strings, 16 inches in length, tuned in pairs to a fifth, the first and second to C, the third and fourth to G, thus—

The compass of the instrument is two octaves.

The frets give the notes in the following manner :—

No. of Fret.	First and Second Strings.	Third and Fourth Strings.
0. [open strings]	C	G
1.	D	A
2.	E	B
3.	F	c
4.	G	d
5.	A	e
6.	c	g
7.	d	a
8.	f	c'

The seventh of the scale is omitted on the first and second strings, the sixth fret giving the octave to the open string. This is characteristic of the tunings of the Chinese Koto, but as the note is given on the third and fourth strings, on which the fourth of the scale is omitted, this is an obvious necessity, as the strings are a fifth apart, and the same fret does duty for both sets of strings. I doubt whether this fact supplies any argument in support of what I think is often stated, that the seventh is omitted in the Chinese diatonic scale.[27]

The music for the Gekkin consists entirely of quaint little Chinese songs, many of them very melodious and pretty. It is played with a small ivory or tortoise-shell plectrum, the double strings giving a trill to the notes, which is accentuated by the vibrations of a wire fastened loosely inside the body : this wire produces a curious jangling whenever the instrument is moved. The up-and-down stroke of the plectrum, which is characteristic of Chinese and Japanese music, acquires additional grace by coming on different strings.*

THE GENKWAN.

The GENKWAN : another Chinese instrument of the same class which has evidently developed out of the Gekkin ; it is without apertures, and contains a wire vibrator in the body. It is played with a small plectrum, to which a long silk cord and tassel are attached, almost identical with that of the Jamisen. It differs from the Gekkin chiefly in its octagonal body and long neck. The sides of the octagon are 4¼ inches, and the measurement from side to side 10 inches. The neck is 2 feet long, and the string-length also 2 feet. In addition to the upper fret, which gives

---

* From Dr. Knott's paper in the " Transactions of the Asiatic Society of Japan "—some of the remarks in which I have already dealt with in my analysis of the scale it appears that there are in Japan two distinct schools of Gekkin players, and that their instruments differ appreciably :—the Nagahara school and the Keian school. From the table of vibrations given, it appears that the differences between the same notes on the two instruments vary from one to four vibrations ; and that the variations from the notes given by the Chinese Gekkin often amount to eighteen vibrations—an almost sufficient proof that the instrument cannot be of much service in determining the true notes of the scale. This table of vibrations is given on page 104.

the open notes, there are eleven frets on the neck and one on the body, giving the full diatonic scale, including the seventh of the scale, which is absent in the lower strings of the Gekkin. The four strings are tuned in pairs to C and G, the compass of the instrument being two octaves and two notes :—[24]

The following instruments, belonging to the Biwa or Gekkin family, are noted in M. Kraus' pamphlet :—

The Kō : an instrument similar to the Genkwan, but with a circular body. It differs essentially from all the other instruments of the class in being richly ornamented with gold lacquer designs. It has four strings and nine frets. The strings do not appear to be tuned in pairs like those of the Gekkin.

The SHUNGA : a very ancient instrument, resembling the Kokyu in the construction of its body, but with five frets on a neck slightly shorter than that of the Gekkin. It is strung with four strings, one of which is much thicker than the rest. It is said to be played by plucking the strings with the fingers, and not with a *bachi* or plectrum. As in the case of the Kū, the strings do not appear to be strung in pairs.

Of the Gekkins also the following varieties are noted.—The " Biwa-shaped Gekkin," with the gourd-shaped body of the Biwa in miniature, strung with four strings tuned in pairs, and eight frets. The " Six-string Gekkin," with six strings tuned in pairs : it has a circular body and sixteen frets, eight of which are set on the body of the instrument and eight on the neck.

The SHIGEN lies midway between the two groups of instruments with frets and instruments without frets. In construction it is allied to the Gekkin, being somewhat larger, and having the octagon body of the Genkwan : it has the vibrating wire but no frets. The disposition of the four strings, however, is that of the Kokyu, the two upper ones being tuned in unison. It is said to be played with the fingers in the manner of the Guitar, and not by plucking the strings.

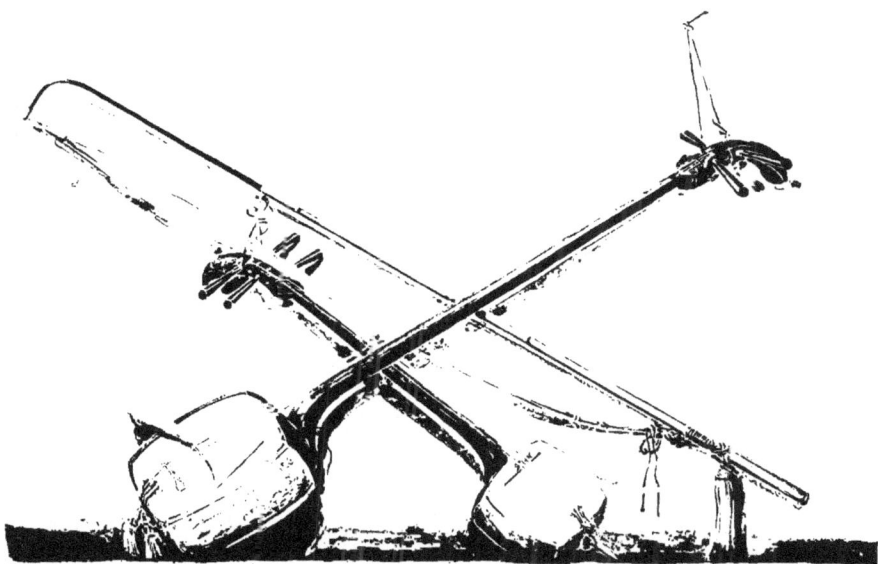

THE SAMISEN AND THE KOKYU

SAMISENS, FIDDLES, AND STRINGED INSTRUMENTS WITHOUT FRETS.

WE come now to a class of instruments of an essentially different type from that of the Biwas and Gekkins. Progress is marked by the disappearance of the frets, the player depending no longer on their aid in producing the different notes, but on the custom which his fingers may acquire in hitting off at once the proper positions for stopping the strings. The cumbersome bodies of the Biwas, and the large faces of the Gekkins, give place to bodies of an altogether different form: in the typical instruments of the family it is an almost square, somewhat shallow box, the sides of wood, the upper and lower surfaces of parchment. This seems to have been developed from a body made of a solid piece of wood. The family may be sub-divided into Samisens, or instruments played with a *bachi*, and Kokyus— those played with a bow.

The SAMISEN. — The instrument as used at the present day is a final development reached by many stages, most of which occurred in China. As has already been said, it was advanced to its present dignity of a national instrument very soon after its advent to Japan from Liu Chiu in 1560: the Biwa players finding it a more portable instrument than their own, and more suited to the accompaniment of lighter songs. The tradition that it had originally two strings only instead of three, as at present, is not supported by the existence of any instrument, as a relic of the past, corresponding with this description. The snake-skin covering to the body is, however, still to be found in some instruments of the family. It has given place now to cat-skin, the value of the parchment being estimated by the number of the nipple marks which are preserved.

There are three tunings, but they have no relation to any system of keys, and are all adapted to *Hirajōshi*, the normal tuning of the Koto.

It is rarely used when the Koto is tuned in any other way, though the possibility of using it is recognised. The three tunings are as follow :—

Honchōshi.

Ni-agari.

San-sagari.

These names would appear to be given to the tunings as a guide to the player, and to enable him to remember what changes have to be made. The use of the words *agari* and *sagari*—" raising " and " lowering "—is somewhat arbitrary, but not entirely unintelligible. *Honchōshi* is the normal *chōshi, joshi,* or tuning ; *Ni-agari*, " the second string raised " ; from F♯ to G♯ ; *San-sagari*, " the third string lowered "—that is, from the octave of the first string G♯, to F♯.

There are also these two special tunings, used only for comic music : —

Ichi-sagari.

San-sa-sagari.

These are named on a similar principle : *Ichi-sagari*, " the first lowered ; " that is, from the octave of the third string C♯, to D♯ ; *San-sa-sagari*, " the third lowered," but this time lowered an octave from the third string—D♯ of the last tuning.

The object of these tunings is curious. They have, as I have said, no relation whatever to changes of key, but are simply selected so that open strings should be used in the piece more frequently than stopped strings, the object being not only to get a clearer vibration, but to ensure greater accuracy by avoiding stopping and the consequent chances of errors. For example, " *Hitotsu-toya* " is played on the Samisen tuned in *Honchōshi*, while for " *Saita Sakurai* " the tuning is *San-sagari*. Both of these pieces would, on the Koto, be played in the same key.

The Samisen is played with a *bachi* of wood, ivory, or tortoise-shell, which strikes the strings just below where the neck joins the body. At this point the face is strengthened with a small extra piece of parchment, which receives the first blow from the *bachi*: there are thus produced two distinct sounds—the drumming on the face, and the vibration of the strings. In the fingering great care is used to let the strings be pressed by the finger-nails.

The measurements of the Samisen are: The body, 7¾ inches long by 7 inches broad, by 3½ inches deep; the neck, 2 feet 5¼ inches long, tapering from 1 inch broad to ⁷⁄₁₀ inch; the pegs, 3 inches long; the *bachi*, 8¼ inches long, rather less than an inch square at the top, and 3½ inches long at the striking edge.

The JAMISEN is a Chinese instrument whose history I have not been able to trace clearly. Although it differs in the construction of its body

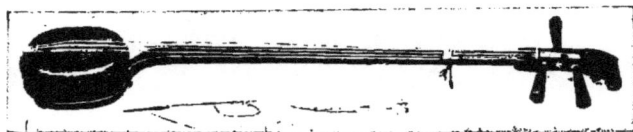

THE JAMISEN.

from the Samisen, it so much resembles that instrument in other respects that there seems very little doubt that they both sprang from the same source. Both front and back of the body of the Jamisen are covered with snake-skin, but instead of being a hollow rectangular frame, like that of the Samisen, the body is an oval block of hard wood, measuring 6 inches in length, 5 in breadth, and 2¾ in thickness, in which a hole 2 inches in diameter is cut. It has three strings, which pass from the tuning pegs, through a small ivory notch on the neck, and over a small ivory bridge on the face; they are fastened to an ivory knob at the base of the belly. The Jamisen is played with a small tortoise-shell plectrum, to which a long silk cord and tassel are attached. The neck is 2 inches shorter than that of the Samisen, but the pegs are much larger. The strings are tuned to *Honchōshi.* [29]

The following varieties of the Samisen are noted by M. Kraus:—

The CHOSEN : identical in construction with the Samisen, but with a much longer neck, measuring about 3 feet 6 inches.

The COREAN SAMISEN : almost identical with the Jamisen, but with a shorter neck and without the small ivory bridge on the face.

The KAOTAKI : an ancient three-stringed instrument from Liu Chiu, with a circular body covered with snake-skin.

The KIRISEN : a similar instrument, with three strings, but with a larger body covered with parchment : it is square, with rounded angles. It is played with the small tortoise-shell plectrum of the Gekkin.

The TAISEN : an enlarged form of the Kirisen, with a circular body, about 15 inches in diameter, covered with parchment. It is played with a small wooden plectrum.

The group of stringed instruments without frets is, as I have said, divided into two classes—those played with a plectrum, and those played with a bow.

In the second class, the Kokyu, or Japanese Fiddle, holds precisely the same position as the Samisen does in the first class : that is to say, it is the ultimate form which has resulted from the innumerable varieties which have preceded it. Its shape is that of the Samisen, but much smaller. It is a four-stringed instrument, almost invariably tuned to *Sansagari* : the third and the fourth strings—the upper and not the lower ones, as with us — are tuned in unison, imparting to the high notes great strength and clearness. It is sometimes, though rarely, tuned to *Honchōshi* and *Ni-agari*. A small wooden rest, with a hole in it for the pivot, fixed in the *obi*, enables the Kokyu to be played by beggars in the street : and when held under the left knee, by foreigners sitting in a chair.

TUNINGS OF THE KOKYU.

San-sagari (normal).

Honchosi.

Ni-agari.

The measurements of the Kokyu are: the body, 5½ inches long, by 4·9 broad, by 2·3 deep; the neck, 18 inches long, its breadth tapering from ·7 to ·6; the pegs, 2½ inches long; the bow, 3 feet 8¼ inches long, with a bend at the upper end 3 inches long; length of horsehair, 2 feet 6½ inches.

The relative sizes of the Samisen and Kokyu are shown in the accompanying illustration. The *bachi* is resting on the face of the Samisen, while the long bow of the Kokyu is hanging above that instrument.

We next come to a group of three curious and somewhat primitive Chinese Fiddles, figured in the accompanying illustration.

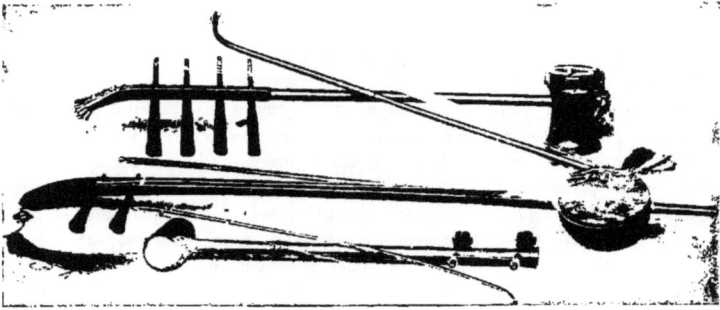

THE KEIKIN, KOKIN, AND TEIKIN.

The KEIKIN: a four-stringed Chinese Fiddle, with a body made of a small segment of bamboo, 5½ inches long by 4 inches in diameter; the neck measures 27 inches. The pegs are 5 inches long, and are placed one below the other, projecting beneath the neck; the strings pass separately through an ivory notch half way down the neck and over a small ivory bridge on the face of the body, the string-length being only 10½ inches. They are tuned in pairs to a fifth, but occasionally also to a fourth.[30] The most curious feature of this instrument is that the horsehair of the bow is twined in and out of the strings, making it impossible

2 A

for a single note to be produced. The bow is 28 inches long. The only fingering which is possible is by pressure on the strings between the lowest peg and the ivory notch: they are then quite close together. The bow is pulled close to the body, on which a lump of resin is stuck. The face of the body is covered with snake-skin, and the back embellished with an open black-wood ornament.

The KOKIN: a two-stringed variety of the Keikin. The body is only 4 inches long by 2 inches in diameter, and the neck, of bamboo, 18 inches long. There is no ivory notch on the neck, but the strings are tied back with a loop of silk. They are, like those of the Keikin, tuned to a fifth, and occasionally to a fourth, the bow being twined in and out of the strings, as in the larger instrument. The face of the body is covered with snake-skin, and the back is uncovered. It has a lump of resin stuck on to it.

The TEIKIN: another form of Chinese Fiddle. It is the same length as the Keikin, but has only two strings, and the pegs project at the side of the neck. The length of the neck is 2 feet 6 inches. The body is spherical in form, and made of black-wood with carved open-work at the back. The face is of lighter wood, 4 inches in diameter. The strings are tuned to a fifth, and pass over a small ivory bridge, to which they come straight from the pegs. The bow is twined in the strings, as in the case of the Keikin and Kokin, and there is, as in the other instruments, a lump of resin on the body.

Two minor varieties in this class alone remain to be noted: the Kokun and the Nisen, the four- and two-stringed Fiddles of Corea. Except that they are somewhat more ornate they correspond in almost all respects with the Keikin and Kokin of China.

It would have been an interesting task to have classified in order of development the whole of this group of stringed instruments, but the necessary materials are wanting.

One general remark alone can be made. There is manifest a desire to produce, by every conceivable combination of mechanical contrivance, every variety of tone of which stringed instruments are capable. The

THE KOKYU-PLAYER.

characteristics of the Biwa are preserved in the Gekkin : they are handed
on and applied to the newer forms of the Samisen, to be afterwards
developed by the Kokyu.

Thus we find the Gekkin and Samisen merged in the Taisen, with its
circular parchment-covered body ; the Kokyu and the Gekkin merged in
the Shunga, with its fretted neck set on a Kokyu body with four strings.
One instrument alone is wanting—a fretted Fiddle : but I am disposed to
think that the Shunga must have been occasionally played with a bow,
although, on the authority of Monsieur Kraus, I have stated that it was
played with the fingers.

FLUTES, AND BAMBOO WIND INSTRUMENTS.

THE Fuyé, or Flute, is said to have originated in North-West Asia, and to have come thence to Japan through China. The Japanese, however, claim their Flute as indigenous to the country. The Chinese Flute is called Ō-teki, or in Japanese, Yokōfuyé —" Side-blowing Flute "— probably to distinguish it from the Hichiriki, which is blown from the end. It is also called Ryūteki—the " Dragon-Flute." It has seven finger-holes, and was made originally of monkey-bone, but afterwards of bamboo. There were two kinds, the long and the short; the latter alone seems to have been in frequent use. It measures 15·5 inches in length; the internal diameter being about ·55 inch, and the lip-hole 10·9 inches, the first finger-hole 6·5, and the last 1·3 from the end. The long variety was made of a thinner bamboo, and produced more delicate notes.

The Japanese Flute, or Yamato-fuyé, is lacquered red inside, and closely bound outside between the holes with string laid on with paste, and afterwards fixed with lacquer. The string is a substitute for strips of the cherry-tree bark which was formerly used, this itself being a sub-stitute for the bark of the Żaba tree of China, with which the old Chinese Flutes were bound. The top is plugged with lead wrapped in rolls of paper fastened with wax, and finished at the end with wood decorated either with brocade or a highly finished metal ornament.

It is difficult fully to appreciate the clear tones of the Japanese Flute, as the notes are seldom blown "clean." Weird quarter-tones disfigure both the beginning and the end of all sustained notes, the musicians being specially taught to acquire the art of producing them; and for some reason, which much enquiry has not revealed to me, the music would be considered as shorn of its beauties if they were omitted.

It has six holes, and measures $17\frac{3}{4}$ inches long, with an internal diameter at the base of slightly less than half an inch. The lip-hole is 12·6 inches, the first finger-hole 7·5, and last 2·7 inches from the end.

The Yamato-fuyé were divided into two classes: the Kagura-fuyé, the measurements of which have just been given, and the Azuma-fuyé, made of a thinner bamboo, and giving a more delicate tone. As their names imply, the former was used in the Kagura orchestra, the latter in that of the Azuma-asobi. In the same way the Chinese Flute is sometimes called the Bugaku-fuyé. The Azuma-fuyé has now given way to the Corean Flute. Koma-fuyé, which is usually carried by the temple musicians with the Kagura-fuyé in a double-barrelled lacquer case.

The Koma-fuyé has six holes, and is made of very thin bamboo, 14½ inches long, with an internal diameter of only ·4 inch. The lip-hole is 9·9 inches, the first finger-hole 5·7, and the last 2 inches from the end.

SEITEKI : a primitive Chinese Flute, used with the Gekkin, Teikin, and Keikin, which are often played together. It is made of plain bamboo,

THE SEITEKI.

unlacquered inside, 21 inches long, with six finger-holes. Its chief peculiarity is that between the upper finger-hole and the lip-hole there is another hole which is covered with paper before the instrument is played, which gives a quaint buzz to the music. At the lower end, also, holes are pierced for a cord and tassel.[31]

The *Encyclopædia* gives two additional forms of Flute :

DŌSHŌ, or "Cave Flute": said to have been much used during the Tong dynasty in China. It measured 2 feet in length. It was originally made as a toy, but was afterwards adopted seriously, and bound with ornamental strings. It was never popular with the Japanese.

CHI : a bamboo Flute with seven holes, said to have been first made about 1000 B.C. The tones resembled a baby's crying, and hence it was never much used.

In Dr. Veeder's paper on Japanese Musical Intervals,[*] the learned author gives the vibration numbers of several different kinds of Flutes and Shakuhachis.

HICHIRIKI : the " Sad-toned Tube " : in appearance and structure this instrument resembles a small Flute, bearing the same proportion to the Flute as the Piccolo does in the West. It is made of bamboo, lacquered inside, and bound with lacquered string, like the Flute, with seven holes above and two thumb-holes below. It is, however, played with a loose reed mouthpiece inserted at one end ; this is bound with paper which, having been damped swells and keeps it firmly in its place. The resemblance to the Piccolo is limited, however, to its size, for the Hichiriki is the diapason of the classical orchestra, and on it must be laid the blame of those sounds, often attributed to the Shō, which are entirely gruesome to Western ears.[32]

THE HICHIRIKI, WITH BOX AND CLEANING ROD.

Hichiriki players are even greater sinners than the flautists in the matter of those superfluous quarter-tones already referred to : the antecedent slur is often a prolonged wailing slide through a full tone, more or less ; the note finishing with an excruciating rise of a semitone, more or less, cut off short. These sounds seem always to have pleased the Japanese ear. The old Hichirikis are as much prized as the old Flutes, their history being recorded with greatest care. It is more correctly kept in a box shaped like a closed fan, but a cover is only an invention of modern times. It measures 7·1 inches long, with an internal diameter

[*] " Transactions of the Asiatic Society of Japan," vol. vii. pt. ii., p. 86.

tapering from ·6 to ·4 of an inch. The first hole is 1·4 inches from the top, the last 1·1 from the bottom. The under holes are 1·9 and 4·1 from the top respectively. The reed mouthpiece – *shita* is 2·3 inches long, but when in place it only projects one inch from the end of the instrument. Special instructions are given for the manufacture of this mouthpiece. It should be made from cane cut at Udono in the province of Yamashiro, in the depth of winter, and dried slowly in the kitchen. It should be bound with the best Mino paper.

The *Encyclopædia* refers to a larger form of the instrument, the Ō-Hichiriki. The only detail given concerning it is that it has nine finger-holes instead of seven.

THE SHAKUHACHI, WITH VERTICAL SECTION

The SHAKUHACHI is made of thick bamboo lacquered inside, measuring from 20 to 20½ inches long. The approximate measurements from joint to joint are 6¼, 5¾, 4, 3½ inches respectively; but in the best instruments these measurements should be 6, 5, 4, 3, inches. The internal diameter measures 1 inch at the top and 1¼ at the base; the external diameter 1½ inch at the top and 2 inches at the base, which is cut so as to include the root-swell of the reed.[33]

Well played it is one of the mellowest of wind instruments ; but the exceeding difficulty of playing it at all justifies the tradition of secrets which have been handed down from Omori Toku, a hermit of Yedo, from generation to generation of patient teachers and patient pupils. The principle of the instrument corresponds with that of an organ pipe, being no more than a hollow tube with a slight cut at the end fitted with a hard ebony " voicing." The under lip of the player almost covers the upper cavity, and thus takes the place of the " language " of the pipe, the breath entering between the edge of the lower lip and the " voicing." It has four upper holes, the centre of the first being 9½ inches from the lip, and a thumb-hole underneath 8½ inches from the lip. By half opening the finger-holes the full Chinese chromatic scale is produced.

The method of playing the Shakuhachi is shown in the engraving of the Kagen-gaku, plate IV., page 18.

There are some small kinds of Shakuhachi, some of them being most elaborately carved.

THE SHŌNO-FUYÉ.

HITOYOKIRI—given by the *Encyclopædia* as a variety of Shakuhachi, a little shorter, but of very sweet sound. It measures 21 inches, and is made out of two joints of bamboo only, the finger-holes coming below the ring, the lip above. The difficulty of finding the necessary bamboo probably accounts for its scarcity.

SHŌNO-FUYÉ: a very ancient instrument, composed of twenty-two pipes, arranged side by side like Pan-pipes. The largest pipe measured 17 inches.

Smaller varieties contained sixteen and twelve pipes respectively.

The Shō (*Shi-yō*), figured on page 188, the primitive mouth-organ, is composed of a compact bundle of seventeen thin bamboo reeds fixed into a circular lacquered wind-chamber of cherry-wood or hard pine, the air passing in a channel round the central support. It is fitted with a silver mouthpiece.[34]

The following are the precise details:—Wind-box : height, 3·4 inches ; diameter, 2·8, which decreases slightly at the base. Projection of silver mouthpiece, ·7 inch ; length, 1·8 ; breadth, 1·1. Rectangular hole in mouthpiece, ·25 by ·6. Height from wind-box of the silver band which holds the reeds in position, 5½ inches.

The reeds are arranged in two sets, those opposite one another being of equal height : each set is also arranged like the front pipes of an organ, the longest in the middle, the remainder getting shorter in couples, one on each side. The longest pipes are in a line with the centre of the mouthpiece ; these are the 4th and the 13th, the first being on the right side. The following diagram shows the arrangement, and also the true pipe-lengths in inches and decimals.

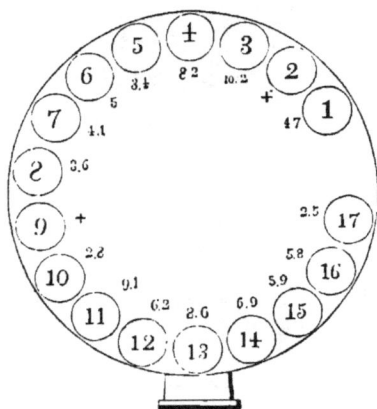

No.	Name of Pipe.	Length.	True Pipe-length.	Note on the Staff.
1	Hii	8·3	4·7	b
2	Mō	10·7	..	..
3	Kotsu	13·5	10·2	A
4	Bok	17·2	8·2	D
5	Jō	13·5	3·4	d
6	Gyō	10·7	5	a
7	Hichi	8·5	4·1	c
8	Gon	5·9	3·6	c♯
9	Ya	5·9	..	..
10	Hechi	8·3	2·8	E
11	Ichi	10·7	9·1	B
12	Bei	13·8	6·2	F♯
13	Kū	17·2	8·6	C♯
14	Otsu	13·5	6·9	E
15	Gei	10·7	5·9	G
16	Jei	8·3	5·8	G♯
17	Sen	5·9	2·5	f♯

In the above table the length of the pipes is given in the third column : and in the fourth column are given the true pipe-lengths—that is to say, the measurements from the upper surface of the wind-box to the bases of the slits made in the pipes, in the same way as the ornamented organ-pipes are treated in the West. These slits are inside, with the exception of those of the 8th and 9th pipes, which are on the outside, and mounted with silver : the tops of the 8th, 9th, and 17th pipes are also silver-mounted : all the others are plain. The 2nd and 9th are dummies.

The pipes are made of the oldest bamboo procurable, much of it being obtained from old country houses ; their internal diameter is ·3. They are closely packed side by side, some of the outer surface being cut away to allow them to fit tightly ; they are inserted into the wind-box to the depth of 1·2 inch. In their bases are fixed small metal reeds, which are silent till the finger-holes are closed : these holes are all one inch from the top of the wind-box, except those of the 6th and 7th pipes, which are 1·9 inch from the top : those of the 14th and 15th pipes are *inside* ; that of the first pipe at the side facing the player. The breath is inhaled very gently, the player having at his side a *hibachi*, over which he occasionally warms the wind-box, to prevent the accumulation of moisture.

The instrument is held to the mouth with both hands, the pipes being disposed among the fingers for stopping as follows :—

> 1st finger, right hand :—14th and 15th pipes, (hole inside), and 1st pipe, with outside of the second joint of the finger.
>
> 2nd finger, right hand :—3rd, 4th, and 5th pipes.
>
> thumb, right hand :—16th and 17th pipes.
>
> thumb, left hand :—8th, 10th, 11th, and 13th pipes.
>
> 1st finger, left hand :—7th pipe.
>
> 2nd finger, left hand :—6th pipe.

THE "BARBARIAN SHŌ."

The first line of the following score gives the notes of the Shō; and the second line gives the chords that occur in music written for the instrument. These are taken from tables prepared by the Educational Department in Tokyo :—

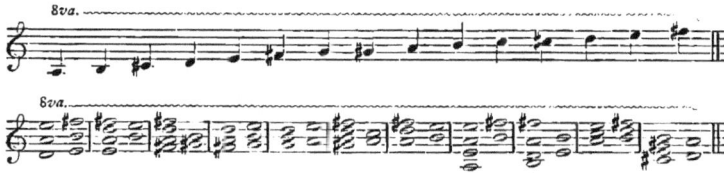

There seem to have been many varieties of the Shō at different periods, varying chiefly in the number of reeds. One is mentioned as having had thirty-six, and others with twenty-six, nineteen, and thirteen respectively. A curious form with a "tea-pot spout" mouthpiece, said to have been called in China the "Barbarian Shō," is figured in Abé Suyenao's "Records," a copy of which is given on the preceding page.

The Shō is probably the oldest Eastern instrument ; the date of its introduction into China being given as the early part of the Chin dynasty, 400 years before the time of Confucius.

THE SHŌ
A IN SITU (PLAN);
B (PLAN)

THE UTA-DAIKO

THE O-TSUZUMI

THE Ō-DAIKO, KOTSUMI, AND TAIBYOSHI

DRUMS.

THE generic name for Drums of all kinds in Japanese is Taiko ; they
are, however, divided into three classes : the Taiko proper, the Kakko,
and the Tsuzumi. But this classification, in the case of the Taiko and
Kakko, is one of nomenclature simply ; a better one may be made which
depends on construction. The three classes will then be—

    I. Plain Cylindrical Drums.
    II. Drums with braces or cords.
    III. Drums with dumb-bell-shaped bodies, or Tsuzumi.

I. PLAIN CYLINDRICAL DRUMS.

Ō-DAIKO : the large Drum, used occasionally in Temple services. It
is generally seen in large Temples standing on the right of the altar ;
it also forms part of the *Dai-dai-kagura* orchestra. It rests on a black
lacquer stand, the surface of the cylinder being usually elaborately decorated
either with gold clouds or coloured dragons, the faces having a large
black "*mitsu-tomoyé*" on a plain ground. In the cylinder are fitted two
large iron rings, which enable it to be carried, as it sometimes, though
rarely, appears in processions. The origin of this Drum, beyond the fact
that it came from China, is not clear. It is said to have been developed
from the Bugaku-daiko (Tsuri-daiko), but the connection between the two,
if it exists at all, would seem to be the other way round.

The faces measure 2 feet 5 inches in diameter, the parchment over-
lapping 5 inches on to the cylinder, to which it is fastened by two rows
of heavy studs. The cylinder is 2 feet 9½ inches long, its section being
slightly convexed, giving a central diameter of 2 feet 10 inches. With
its stand the height is 4 feet 10 inches.

KO-DAIKO : a small form of Ō-daiko, used chiefly in processions, and
in the orchestra for some of the shorter performances of the *Kagura*.

The cylinder of the orchestral Drum is decorated, and it rests on a stand ; the processional Drum is plain ; in both cases the faces are undecorated.   It is placed in a cubical frame suspended from a pole carried on the shoulders of two men, the drummer walking by the side delivering vigorous blows on the parchment with two plain thick sticks of hard wood without knobs or leather : these sticks are about one foot in length and over an inch and a half in diameter.   Before the procession starts it is placed at the Temple gate, where it is beaten continuously for two hours or more to summon the people.   Either this Drum, or a smaller variety, was formerly used in battle.

The faces measure 1 foot 10½ inches in diameter, the parchment over-lapping 3½ inches.   The convexed cylinder is 2 feet 2½ inches in length, with a central diameter of 2 feet 4½ inches. · With its stand the height is 3 feet 11 inches.   The stand, however, is occasionally much higher, as in the Temple of the second Tokugawa Shōgun at Shiba.

Tsuri-daiko — the "Hanging Drum" — more commonly called simply Taiko : the larger of the two Drums used in the Bugaku orchestra. It is a shallow cylinder very slightly convexed, hung in a circular rim or frame on a stand, and so arranged as to height that the drummer sitting in front of this instrument may, without the slightest stretching of his arm, strike the exact centre of the face.   The sticks have leather-covered knobs, and measure only 11 inches in length ; when not in use they are placed in rings at the side of the frame.   The right stick is called *obachi* — the male stick : the left *mebachi* — the female stick.   Both faces and the cylinder are elaborately painted in the usual style of Temple decoration, the phœnix or the dragon surrounded by gorgeous clouds.   The stand and frame are richly lacquered, and terminate with the *kwa-yen* — the flame ornament — and balls of fire, made in brass.   In tone the Drum is very full and mellow.   Its use in the orchestra is to mark the larger divisions of the time — the *hyōshi* — which are practically equivalent to the Western bars.[35]

On very great occasions a much larger Drum — Da-daiko — is used ; but this belongs properly to the second, or "braced" class.

The Tsuri-daiko varies slightly in size ; its average dimensions, how-ever, are as follow : Diameter of face, 20 inches ; diameter of circular

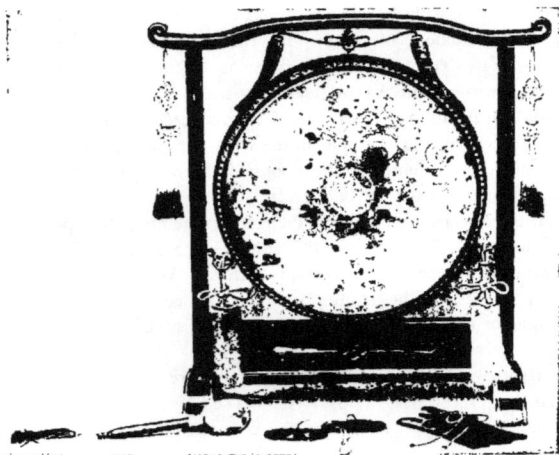

THE TSURI-DAIKO (Seen from behind), AND KAKKO.

frame, 32 inches, the rim being two inches broad and one inch thick. The cylinder is only 8 inches long. The height from the floor to the top of the *kwa-yen* ornament is 4 feet 3 inches.

In the illustrations on the preceding page two varieties of Tsuri-daiko are given : in the upper one is shown the form here described ; in the lower, a form sometimes found for the secular orchestra. The different shape of the single stick will be noticed. The other instruments shown in the plates will be described in due course.

Very special instructions are given for playing this Drum. As will be seen in the analysis of the time of Bagaku music, given after the description of the Kakko, a loud drum point with the " male " is invariably preceded by a soft beat with the " female " stick. The position of the sticks at the time of striking is indicated in the following illustration :—

KERŌ : a small Drum used in China, according to the old records, about the period of the Tong dynasty, to signalize the appearance of dawn ;

THE KERŌ.

it is now used in Japan for the purpose of marking the time in processional orchestras. It is hung round the leader's neck by a cord, which he holds in his left hand, together with the rattle, Furi-tsuzumi, beating the *hyōshi* with the stick in the right hand. The face measures only 6½ inches in diameter, with a cylinder 6 inches long, the sides slightly convexed, giving a central diameter of 7½ inches. The faces are silvered, with black "*mitsu-tomoyé*," and are fastened on to the gilt cylinder by gilt studs, the parchment overlapping as in the large Drums of the class.

II. DRUMS WITH BRACES.

The chief characteristic of this class is that the faces have a larger diameter than the cylinder, giving roughly the following section :—

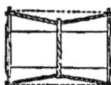

The braces or "snares," generally of thick silk or hemp cords, run through holes cut in the rims of the faces, as in the dotted lines in the diagram, and are drawn tight by a central cord.

DA-DAIKO : the large Drum used only on the greatest occasions in the Bugaku orchestra instead of the Tsuri-daiko. It is erected on a special plat-form, draped and tasseled, with a gold railing and steps. The drummer, who is specially selected for his skill, stands in front of the Drum, the directions being that he should, for greater vigour in striking, place his left foot on the platform, and his right on the upper step. It is surrounded with a broad rim ornamented with phœnix and dragon, and edged with red *kwa-yen*, or "flames." This frame is fixed into a socket in the plat-form. The whole is surmounted by a black lacquer pole, 7½ feet in length, which supports a gold sun more than a foot in diameter, with rays 18 inches long. The faces are gilt, and bear in front a black "*mitsu-tomoyé*," and at the back a "*futatsu-tomoyé*." The cylinder is richly decorated on red lacquer ; the hemp braces are black, white, and red, and are nearly an inch in diameter.

The diameter of the faces is about 6 feet 3 inches ; the length of the cylinder 5 feet, with diameter 4 feet 2 inches, the wood of which it is composed being 2¾ inches thick. The Drum is not fastened to the pole, as appears in the accompanying sketch, but rests on a stand, which is shown in a separate cut. The cylinder is provided with two "ears," which serve as handles. The form of the internal supports of the case of the body is also shown in the illustrations.

The description and rough sketches of this huge Drum are taken from Suyenao's "MS. Records of Ancient Music," the Drums themselves being exceedingly rare. The two belonging to the Temples at Nikko are hopelessly broken ; another, sent to the Vienna Exhibition in 1873, suffered shipwreck, and still lies at the bottom of the sea.

Ni-daiko—the "Portable" Drum, figured on page 197 : a smaller processional variety of the Da-daiko. It is carried by a black lacquer pole, eight feet long, on the shoulders of two men ; the drummer, as in the case of the Ko-daiko, walking by the side. The tone is very poor and thin. Its gilt faces with black "*mitsu-tomoyé*," red lacquer body, and coloured strings, correspond with those of the larger Drum. It has, however, no outer rim, and is merely surmounted by one red flame, 15 inches high by 20 broad. The diameter of the faces is 2 feet 7 inches ; the cylinder is 1 foot 3 inches long, and 1 foot 8 inches in diameter.

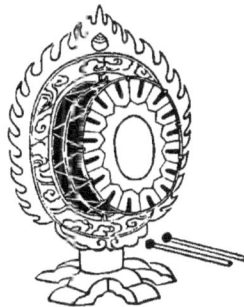

THE HAPPU.

Happu : a very old Chinese Drum filled with rice-powder. It was similar in shape to the Ni-daiko, but was hung in a circular frame on a

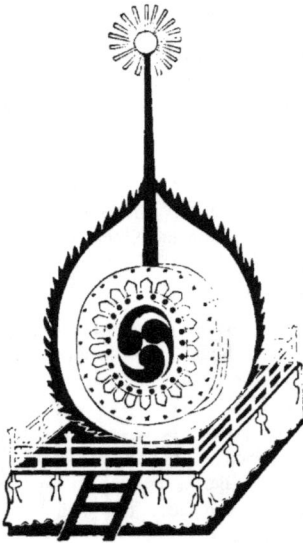

THE DA-DAIKO ON ITS PLATFORM.

ONE SIDE OF THE KWA-YEN FRAME OF THE DA-DAIKO.

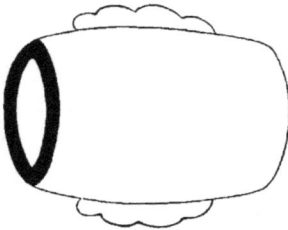

CYLINDER OF THE DA-DAIKO.

INTERNAL SUPPORT OF CYLINDER.

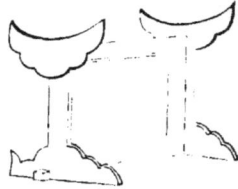

CYLINDER STAND OF THE DA-DAIKO.

THE NI-DAIKO ON ITS POLE.

The DA-DAIKO and NI-DAIKO (*from sketches in Abé Suyenao's "MS. Records of Ancient Music"*).

stand embellished with flame ornament like the Tsuri-daiko, and was probably about the same size. The figure in the cut on page 196 is taken from the *Encyclopædia*.

KAKKO (figured in the upper engraving on page 193): described in the *Encyclopædia* "the Barbarian Drum which came through China from Turkestan and Thibet." It is the small Drum of the Bugaku orchestra; it is, nevertheless, the leader of that orchestra, its function being to mark the "beats" of the music. It is composed of a painted wooden cylinder, 1 foot long, and 6·2 inches in diameter, with a parallel section. The projecting faces are 10 inches in diameter: these faces are painted white. The Drum is braced eight times with thick silk cords. It rests on a small stand in front of the player, the height of the whole being 15 inches; the sticks are unpadded, 15½ inches long, and knobbed like those of the Western Kettle-drum.

It is struck in three different ways:

Katarai: a number of quick strokes with the left stick, slightly increasing in speed.

Mororai: a number of alternate strokes with both sticks, also increasing in speed, making a slow roll.

Sei: a single tap with the right stick.

The stroke is a circular motion, figured in the "Records of Ancient Music" as a "*tomoye*," thus:

MOTION OF LEFT STICK.   MOTION OF RIGHT STICK.

Bugaku music is divided into bars—*hyōshi*—which are each subdivided into divisions or beats, called *kobyōshi;* the half-beat of each *kobyōshi* is called *kagé*—corresponding with the "and" in Western counting. *Katarai,* or *mororai,* exactly fills one of the full beats, and as the time is about *alla breve,* the length of each roll can easily be estimated.

There are three species of time— *yo-hyōshi* or *shi-hyōshi,* containing four beats, the common time; *ya-hyōshi* or *hachi-hyōshi,* with eight beats; and *mu-hyōshi* or *roku-hyōshi,* with six.

The conclusion of every *hyōshi* is marked by a tap on the Kakko (*sei*), and a *forte* stroke on the Taiko with the right stick (*obachi*), which is itself prepared by a *piano* stroke with the left stick (*mebachi*) at the half-beat immediately preceding it : in the common time at "three and."

It will thus be seen that the rhythm of this music differs from Western music in working up to its accent, instead of starting with it.

The emphasis of the dance follows naturally the accent of the music, the drum-point being marked by the stamp of the foot with which those who have seen these dances are familiar.

Ku, the places where the singers take breath, correspond with the *kobyōshi*.

These explanations will be sufficient to explain the following scheme of the different "times," which governs both the music with, and that without, the Drums :—

YO-HYŌSHI [the bar of 4 beats.]	*Beat.*	*Kakko.*		*Tsuri-daiko.*	
	1.	mororai			
	2.	sei			
	3.	katarai			
	and		*kagé*	mebachi	(*Piano*)
	4.	sei		obachi	(*Forte*)
YA-HYŌSHI [the bar of 8 beats.]	1.	mororai			
	2.	mororai			
	3.	mororai*			
	4.	sei			
		katarai †			
	5.	sei			
	6.	sei			
		katarai			
	7.	sei			
	and		*kagé*	mebachi	
	8.	sei		obachi	
MU-HYŌSHI [the bar of 6 beats.]	1.	mororai			
	2.	mororai			
	3.	mororai			
	and	katarai			
	4.	sei			
		katarai			
	5.	sei			
	and		*kagé*	mebachi	
	6.	sei		obachi	

* This is not continuous roll for three beats ; the *mororai* recommences at each beat.
† *Katarai* follows the *sei* immediately.

In addition to these a mixed time—*Tadatyōshi*—is sometimes, though rarely, used, which contains three beats. In this there are no rolls on the Kakko.

1st *hyōshi*	1		sei		
*		and		*kagé*	
	2		sei		
		and		*kagé*	
	3			*kagé*	mebachi
		and		*kagé*	
2nd *hyōshi*	1		sei		obachi
		and		*kagé*	
	2		sei		
		and		*kagé*	
	3			*kagé*	mebachi
		and		*kagé*	
3rd *hyōshi*	1		sei		obachi

D.C. from ✦

The full time of *Tadatyōshi* contains four *hyōshi*, which are all alike, except that the *forte* beat on the big Drum on the first beat of the bar does not occur in the first bar ; and the last bar is incomplete, containing only the *obachi* beat. The cycle of four bars is ranked as a species of *Va-hyōshi*.

DAIBYOSHI, sometimes called Ō-Kakko : a large form of Kakko used in the Kagura orchestra. Its dimensions are : diameter of face, 1 foot 6·5 inches, with a gold band 3 inches broad, and an inner black band about ·625 inch broad ; length, 1 foot 6·75 inches : diameter of the cylinder, 11 inches. It rests on a small stand, the whole standing 2 feet 2·75 inches from the ground. It is strung with 12 braces, and is struck with plain sticks, without knobs, 1 foot 10 inches long. The Drum is figured on page 189.

The name, the "grand time beater," signifies the instrument used to mark the beats on special occasions. When the short benedictory dance, the modern Kagura, is performed at festivals, this Drum is always used to mark the *hyōshi*.

KAIKO : "an enlarged and shortened Kakko," not now in use. According to the "Records of Ancient Music" it was called "the third processional instrument," the Ni-daiko and the Ni-shōko probably being the first and the second. It was carried on the left shoulder, and struck or rubbed with the fingers of the right hand, the beating being accompanied by short shouts, which, it is said, caused the instrument to be disliked. The face, painted white, measured 14 inches in diameter : the length of the cylinder was

6·5 inches, with a diameter of 10 inches. It was painted red, and decorated in the usual elaborate manner; the thick red cords formed eight braces.

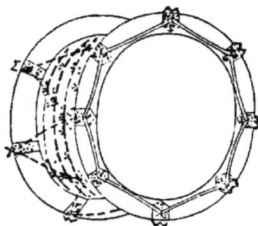

THE KAIKO.

UTA-DAIKO, the "Song-Drum"; commonly called Shimé-daiko, the "Tied-Drum"; and also Geza-daiko, the Drum of the *geza* theatres. It is the commonest of the Japanese Drums, and is used in the theatres, in the orchestra of Sarugaku, and on many other occasions. In shape it resembles the Kaiko, its dimensions being practically the same. The painted body of the Chinese Drum gives place, however, to one of plain *kiri* wood, and the white face to one of plain parchment with a black lacquer border 1·5 inch wide. It is played with two plain sticks without knobs, but with the sharp edges bevelled off. The Drum is placed in front of the player in a wooden frame, which gives it a slight forward inclination, so that the lower edge of the instrument is 7·5 inches high, the upper 11 inches. It seems to have been first played about 1540 A.D. by Komparu Gon-no-kami, a Taiko player in the Court band, and one of the famous house of Komparu. The cords are, as usual, orange-red; but the dignity of the pale blue and lilac cords used formerly to be conferred on the celebrated players.

The Uta-daiko appears in many of the illustrations of this work. The front view is shown on page 188, the back view in the following illustration.

The illustrations of the different orchestras, on pages 27 and 33, indicate the very vigorous action of the drummer, and the position of the Drum on the floor in front of him. Both the sticks are lifted over the right shoulder and brought down with a rapid circular motion on to the face of the Drum, and immediately raised into position again for the next stroke.

2 D

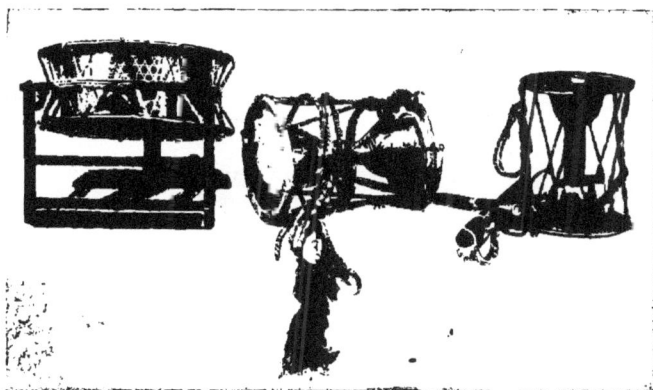

THE UTA-DAIKO, THE O-TSUZUMI, THE KO-TSUZUMI, AND THE KAGURA-FUYÉ.

III. DRUMS WITH DUMB-BELL-SHAPED BODIES—TSUZUMI.

This class of Drums seems to be really a modification of the Kakko. They have overlapping faces, but a curious dumb-bell-shaped body has been substituted for the straight cylinder. The bell-shaped ends of the body are hollow. These Drums came to Japan from China, but, like the Kakko, are not of Chinese origin; it is said that they were used by the Barbarians 1,000 years before the time of Confucius to accompany the worship of the Gods. In Japan their chief use is to supply the place of the Kakko when the orchestra is standing.

The body is red, and highly decorated; the leather face painted white, with eight metal-faced holes for the red cords. It is struck with black sticks 1 foot long.

The Drum is made in three sizes.

ICHI-NO-TSUZUMI, or IKKO : the face, 8 inches in diameter; length of cylinder, 14 inches ; and diameter where it meets the face, 6 inches.

NI-NO-TSUZUMI: mention of this Drum is to be found only in ancient records– it is now never used. Its dimensions were: diameter of face, 10 inches; length of cylinder, 16 inches; and diameter. 7½ inches.

SAN-NO-TSUZUMI: used only for "Koma," or Corean music. Its dimensions are not given, but are probably: diameter of face, 12 inches; length of cylinder, 18 inches; and diameter, 9 inches.

From this Chinese Drum the Japanese variety was invented by the Crown Prince Umayado in the reign of the Empress Suiko, at the beginning of the eighth century. The Japanese Drums are of two sizes, both smaller than the Ikko; the cords are grasped tightly in the left hand, and the Drum struck with the right, the larger being held over the left thigh, the smaller over the right shoulder, the musician sitting in the usual Japanese position.

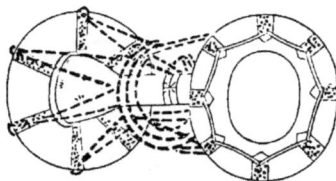

THE NI-NO-TSUZUMI.
(From a sketch in the "Records of Ancient Music.")

OTO-TSUZUMI, or KO-TSUZUMI: the "Younger," or shoulder-drum. Diameter of face, 8 inches; length of body, 10 inches; diameter at ends, 3·5 inches; and in the centre, 1·5 inches.

E-TSUZUMI, or Ō-TSUZUMI: the "Elder," or side-drum. Diameter of face, 8·75 inches; length of body, 11·5 inches; diameter at ends, 4 inches, and in the centre, 2 inches.

The faces of the side-drum are plain: those of the shoulder-drum have black lacquer rims, one ring inside, and trefoil ornaments at the six holes through which the cords pass.

The red body of the Chinese Drum is replaced by one of black lacquer with gold decoration, and the parchment faces are unpainted. The only difference in the structure of the body is, that the centre part of the dumb-bell is moulded in the Japanese Drums, and has a parallel section in the Chinese.

Yamato and Kyōto produced the most famous Drum makers. The colour of the silken cords denotes the grade of the musician : the ordinary colour is orange-red, the next rank has light-blue, and the highest lilac. This rule applies also to the Uta-daiko.

The function of the Drum in the orchestra was to mark and empha-size the rhythm of the dance : the orchestra of the later Nō often contains one side- and three shoulder-Drums : they are tuned together, but they do not necessarily play all together

The tone is much fuller than might be expected, more especially that of the O-tsuzumi, which is struck with more vigorous strokes than the shoulder-drum.

GONGS.

SHŌKO : the Gong of the Bugaku orchestra, and the first metal instrument introduced into Japan. It is shown by the side of the Tsuri-daiko, in the upper plate on page 193. In China it dates from a little later than the time of Confucius. It is said that until brass instruments were made in Japan it was used in the place of a bugle for the words of command. It is of bronze, saucer-shaped, and measures 5·5 inches in diameter, and ·75 inch in depth : it is struck with two very hard knobbed sticks 18 inches long (figured on page 207), joined by a cord, giving a very acute sound. It is used to emphasize the *hyōshi* beat of the Tsuri-daiko, the authorities on the ancient dancing saying that it is always struck immediately after the big Drum. It is suspended by orange silk cords from a lacquer stand resembling in form that of the Taiko, but with a proportionately longer stem : it stands 2 feet 5½ inches from the ground, the player sitting in front of it in the usual Japanese position. The diameter of the circular part of the stand is 11 inches, the rim being 1½ inch broad by ¾ inch thick.

There are two larger sizes of Shōko, corresponding with the two large-sized Drums, Ni-daiko and Da-daiko, with which they are respectively used. Both the Ni-shōko and the Dai-shōko are exceedingly rare instruments, and not often seen ; I have, therefore, again had recourse to the " Records of Ancient Music," already referred to, for the illustrations on page 207.

DAI-SHŌKO : the "Grand Shōko" ; used to accompany the Da-daiko. Like the Drum, it stands on a special platform with its steps, draperies, and tassels. This platform is 2 feet high and 3 feet 7 inches square ; the railing 9 inches high. The Gong is 14 inches in diameter : it is gilt, and has the usual frame of *kwa-yen*, which fits into a socket into the platform : the frame is 5 feet high, and 3 feet broad at the base.

NI-SHŌKO : the " Portable Shōko" ; carried by two men on a long pole, and used to accompany the Ni-daiko in processions. It is gilt, and has an elaborate frame of clouds and fire, measuring 3 feet 5 inches in height by

2 feet wide. The black lacquer pole is 7 feet long, and the Gong 8 inches in diameter.

KEI, or HOKYO: the Temple Gong, which stands on a table at the right of the altar. It is of solid metal three-fifths of an inch thick, and is often gilt, being suspended by curiously interlaced silk cords from a lacquer stand 2 feet 3 inches high by 1 foot 10 inches broad: it is struck with a very hard knobbed stick, 1 foot long, and gives a lower and mellower note than the Shōko.

. There are various shapes, but they may all be roughly described as a truncated half lozenge.

THE KEI.

The length of the gilt Kei in use in the Nikkō Temples (shown in the accompanying illustration) is 8·5 inches at the top and 10·75 at the bottom, with an average breadth of 4·5 inches.

A smaller and thinner variety, in plain bronze, measures 6·75 inches at the top, 9·25 at the bottom, with an average breadth of 3·25 inches. Both forms of the Kei are given on page 212.

DŌBACHI: the "Copper Cup." The large cup-shaped Gong used in the Temples, and also given on page 212. It is placed on a cushion on a lacquer stand, and struck with a short stick covered with leather. The best tone is produced by an upward stroke, the stick just catching the rim of the Gong. It is called Keisu by some sects, who use it instead of the Kei.

The tone of the Dōbachi is exceedingly beautiful, and I can only regret that I have no information to give my readers as to the composition of

THE DAI-SHŌKO ON ITS PLATFORM.

FRAME OF KA-ME OF DAI-SHŌKO.

STICKS OF THE SHŌKO.

THE NI-SHŌKO ON ITS POLE.

The DAI-SHŌKO and NI-SHŌKO (*from sketches in Abé Suyenao's "Records of Ancient Music"*).

the metal. I believe however, that a considerable amount of silver is mixed with the copper.

The following instruments are taken chiefly from the Encyclopædia, " *Sansai Zuyé* " :—

DOKO : a small brass or copper Gong from Southern China, hung on a stand, and generally arranged n a set of three.

KEN : a small Gong originally made of porcelain, the size of a goose's egg. It was pierced with six holes, and was tapped with a stick.

KURE-TSUZUMI : a wooden ng, struck with sticks, from Southern China.

HU : a teacup-shaped porcelain Gong. Its use was suggested by the sound of drinking cups when accidentally struck.

Shôkʋ : a box of wood or metal, 2 feet 5 inches by 1 foot 10 inches. A movable clapper is fixed inside, with which the player struck the sides of the box.

Môku-gyo— the "Wooden Fish": a wooden Gong used in the Temples, struck with a padded stick. It was formerly shaped like a fish bent backwards with its tail in its mouth : it now takes the shape of a bird in the same position. It will be seen in the picture of the Dôbachi, on page 212, lying by the side of the stand.

Dora : the ordinary Gong, which has been adopted in the West. It was originally used in China by the night watchmen.

Waniguchi —the "Shark's Mouth" Gong : the gilt Gong which hangs at the entrance of the shrines. It is struck by worshippers by means of a rope hanging in front of it. It is shown on page 212.

Gyo : a hollow wooden figure of a recumbent tiger, one foot long. It was struck with a small broom or split bamboo.

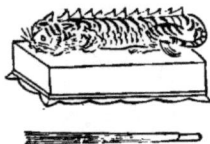

Dô-byôshi : brass Cymbals of different sizes. These Cymbals are also shown lying in front of the Tsuri-daiko in the lower picture on page 193.

2 E

The name, like that of the Drum Dai-byōshi, indicates its use, which is to mark the *hyōshi* of the dance ; they are the " Copper Time-beaters."

HYŌSHIGI : two hard wood Clappers, used on a variety of occasions. In the Theatre they are beaten on the floor rapidly to emphasize confusion.

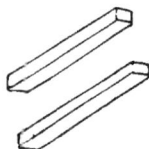

The conductors of juggling, athletic, and other performances, use them to attract attention ; also the night-watchmen during their perambulations of the streets. The word *hyōshi* again appears ; these are the " Wooden Time-beaters."

BYAKUSHI : nine long tablet-shaped pieces of hard wood strung together, used as Clappers. They are now made of bamboo.

YOTSUDAKE—the " Four Bamboos " : Clappers like the preceding, used at the Theatre, and by beggars.

HAKU-HAN : another form of wooden Clapper, shown by the side of the Tsuri-daiko in the lower picture on page 193.

Furi-tsuzumi — the "Shaking Drum," or Tōko: a Rattle used in processions. It is composed of two miniature Drums, about 3 inches in diameter, and 4 inches in length, placed at right-angles, one on top of the other, at the end of a stick about 20 inches long. Five or six little bell Rattles are hung on the Drums by short strings. The faces of the Drums are silvered, with black "*mitsu-tomoyé*" painted on them, and are surrounded by a row of gilt studs. The bodies are red, and elaborately ornamented; the stick is painted red and black, and terminates with a gilt spear-head

3 inches above the Drums. The Rattle is held by the leader of the processional band with the small Drum Kerō.[36]

Suzu : the Rattle used by the scarlet-robed dancing ladies of the Temples, when performing their benedictory dance. It is shown on page 212.

Fūrin — the "Wind Bell," shown with the Kei on page 212 : a Bell with a broad flat clapper coming below the body of the Bell, which catches the wind. Occasionally streamers were tied to the clappers. The Fūrin is usually suspended at the four corners of the eaves of the Temples.

MOKKIN : thirteen wooden tablets fixed on a frame or hollow box with
handles, somewhat in the form of a Western Harmonicons. It measures
22 inches long by 9 inches high by 9 inches broad.   It is played with two
knobbed sticks.

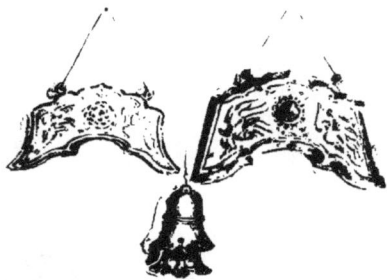
THE KEI IN TWO FORMS, AND THE RÖKIN

THE ŌGACHI AND MOKU-GYO

THE WANIGUCHI

THE SUZU

BRASS.

RAPPA: a brass Bugle used in camp; sometimes called the "Foreigner's Flute."

DŌKAKU: another Bugle, made of copper, and formerly of wood.

CHARUMERA: a Bugle with holes, which is used occasionally in the Theatre, but chiefly by the itinerant vendors of sweets in Japan. Its sounds, and the tunes played on it, have many affinities with those of the Italian *Pifferari*. Both the Charumera and Dōkaku are said to be much used in Corea as processional instruments.

THE RAPPA.   THE DŌKAKU.   THE CHARUMERA.

NOTES.

By T. L. SOUTHGATE.

1 [*Page* 2].—It should be noted that the early stringed instruments, from the types of those used by the ancient Egyptians down to the instruments employed in Europe till the seventeenth century, were also of a sweet, but feeble, quality of tone. Owing to the shape of the instruments of the Viol family, notably their flat backs, they lacked resonance; with the improvements of the great Cremonese makers they gained in power. The same may be observed of the ancient Harp, which, owing to its having no front pillar to resist the tension of the strings, could only have given forth faint sounds, probably not so loud as those drawn from the Lutes and Theorbos of our ancestors. And much the same may be said of the Clavichord, Virginal, Spinet, and Harpsichord, the precursors of the Pianoforte; the tone of all these instruments was sweet but very feeble in comparison with that evoked from a sonorous "Broadwood" of to-day. Oddly enough, just the converse is true of the wind reed instruments. These were all much more powerful and less under control than those in use to-day. Of the wind family in general the Flute no doubt was softer, but the brass and all the others must have been much louder than are their modified descendants now used.

2 [*Page* 6].— In that the Japanese musicians produce some effects different from those obtained by Western musicians, it is evident that our system of notation is not available to include all that these Eastern musicians do. In early times, music, like ancient poetry, and like the religious liturgies, was oral, and not written down: it was carried on from age to age by tradition. The history of musical notation teaches us that, with the gradual development of the art, the capabilities of representing it in signs grew with the advance of the music itself. A full score of to-day, representing in definite characters our tone-language, would excite the wonderment of the old Greek priests, who chanted their hymns to Bacchus from the single signs of their alphabet (variously arranged), quite as much as would the elaborate music itself given forth by our orchestras of to-day. The art of writing has been characterised as the greatest invention mankind has made; the art of setting down signs to represent sounds is just as wonderful. It is quite certain that, if the necessity arises, it will be possible to write in an intelligible notation any effects that may be produced by nations using a system of music differing from that of our own.

3 [*Page* 7].—The fact that the music for the Koto is learnt by rote, rather than by being taught through notation, would seem to point to the great antiquity of the instrument. This was the mode of instruction the players went through in the Egyptian temples ages ago; and, indeed, it may be pointed out that in early Christian times, the pneumes in which the chant was set down were regarded rather as aids to memory, than as signs which exactly represented the pitch and duration of the notes to be sung.

4 [*Page* 13].—We have a somewhat analogous example in the Western world to this temporary migration of musical pupils. The early Egyptian school of music was so famous, that, according to Diodorus Sicculus, the Greek musicians went to Alexandria to obtain instruction, and occasionally famous natives of Egypt came to Athens and Corinth to give performances. Pythagoras, who may be looked upon as the father of scientific music in Greece, obtained all his knowledge of the art during his long residence in the Land of the Pharaohs. This happened about a thousand years before Japan sent her students in music to study in Corea or China.

5 [*Page* 18].—It may be noted that Dancing is still a part of the ritual of the Abyssinian Church, which professes to have derived this ceremony from the ancient Jewish Church— " David danced before the Lord." In the Abyssinian ritual, the Dance is accompanied by Bells and Drums. In our Western Church, the custom still lingers at Seville, where the late Sir Frederick Gore Ouseley relates he once saw a solemn Fandango danced in front of the high altar.

6 [*Page* 18].—This reminds one of the famous collection of the "Cantigas de Santa Maria," a remarkable set of songs with music of the 13th century, preserved in the library of the Escurial.

7 [*Page* 20].—Such was the ancient Lyre of the Greeks, an instrument of open strings and having no finger-board; and coming to later times, such was the Italian "Accordo," an instrument possessing twelve strings, and used mainly for accompanimental purpose, though its neck was fretted, and various intervals could be played on each string.

8 [*Page* 22].—It is a little curious to note that in the Middle Ages we also had three sets of people dealing with music—the performers in the Church, engaged with sacred music; the teachers in the Universities, who composed academic music; and the more popular minstrels, who played and sang for the public, and were quite unable to read or write music.

9 [*Page* 23].—Analogous examples of trade cries existed with us until within the last few years. In ancient Egypt, trade songs and cries were rigorously protected, and many such distinctive public street cries are still common in the East.

10 [*Page* 45].—The appreciation of music in its different systems resembles that of language. It is mainly a matter of where we are born, and what we have been accustomed to hear from infancy. The music current among some other races is unintelligible to us, just as their language is. The system with which we are familiar seems to us the only perfect and intelligible one. Our Western method is both melodic and susceptible of harmony; but it is not wise to despise other systems just because we do not understand and are not familiar with them. Nor is it safe to say that they are only melodic, and incapable of harmonic treatment. The resources of harmony are not yet exhausted; and though it seems a fundamental truth to rely on the statement that our scalar division of the octave is founded on Nature's acoustic laws, it is certain that our system is not mathematically correct so far as the division of intervals is concerned: we have to temper them for purposes of harmony and combination. There is no valid reason to prove that other scalar divisions are not also practicable for harmonic as well as melodic purposes.

11 [*Page* 69].—That public examinations for degrees in music and diplomas are held under authorisation is proof of the great importance in which the art is regarded in Japan. The very long study it requires, and the slow progress made in it, are evidences of the abundant leisure which everyone seems to enjoy in that country. It seems that everything must be done thoroughly, and each step completely mastered, before a fresh advance is taken—a very different state of things from that which exists here, where bogus institutions, intent on fee-gathering, are too ready to issue degrees and diplomas for payment, combined with very little knowledge or proficiency.

12 [*Page* 88].—The history of the scale, or series of sounds, employed by the Japanese in their music, is so obscure, that an attempt to unravel its origin and trace its development would probably result in adding little to our knowledge. The scale was no doubt derived from Chinese sources, and its chief interest for us lies in its present capacity of expression. So far as we are able to determine by hearing their music and examining the tunings of their instruments, and apart from the scientific testing of the individual sounds by means of a syren or a graduated monochord, the notes employed by the Japanese do not materially differ from the sounds we use. They may not be mathematically the same as our tempered system, so far as the exact number of their individual vibrations is concerned, but they are practically identical with our diatonic and chromatic scales. In all probability the Japanese have had no mathematicians able to determine the vibration-number of the notes and their ratios to one another, nor do they seem acquainted with the acoustic laws of harmonics on which the Western system of chord-construction is founded, yet their musicians have arrived at much the same result as obtains with us. The question is one of much interest, because among the near neighbours of the Chinese are the Hindoos, and in the not far south the Maories. Carl Engel and Captain C. H. Day have pointed out that these nations employ a scale containing many more sounds in the octaves than those used by us; while the Javanese, according to Mr. W. Ellis, divide their octave into five exactly equal parts. Yet the Japanese system is allied to the Western method, and the Eastern systems of their nearer neighbours are ignored.

In one respect the Japanese follow the Eastern plan of slurring up or down to a note instead of taking it firmly; this occurs chiefly in their vocal music, but it has caused musical visitors to declare that they sing out of tune, and use minuter intervals than ours. This declaration is founded on as erroneous an assumption as it would be to declare that our string-instrument players did the same when they slurred up to a note, or to censure a vocalist for singing out of tune when passing insensibly from the leading note to the tonic at the close of a song. We must admit that the Japanese know of and use all our intervals, but the haphazard sort of way they select the notes to tune their strings to, and the fact that the systematised scale we accept as a logical ladder of sounds is not recognised by them, and that in much of their music some notes find no place, have caused investigators to come to the conclusion that the Japanese scale is an imperfect one. This is as much an error as it would be to assume that a piece of modern music, deliberately written without employing the fourth or seventh of the scale, did not belong to our diatonic method. We cannot judge of what intervals a scale is composed merely by the tuning of certain strings, neither can we say that a system is truncated because we find tunes in which some notes are omitted. The duty of the Japanese musician is to learn to play tunes; he only concerns himself with the notes necessary for each tune in the scale, *quâ* scale, and is indifferent to anything more. He looks at the music from an emotional rather than from a scientific point of view; hence, Western musicians, with their fuller knowledge, are better able to analyse and reduce Japanese music to its elements than are the native musicians themselves.

2 F

13 [*Page* 97].—The different tunings of the Kotos, Biwas, and Samisens, seem arbitrary and unmeaning to us, and in investigating Japanese music there is a danger that we may confound the tuning with the scale; but the two things are quite distinct. We can no more judge of what the scale is like from the tuning of these instruments, than we can assert that the different notes employed for the lowest strings of the Violin, Viola, Violoncello, and Double-bass, or the Pianoforte and Organ, form the tonic foundation on which the scales of these instruments rest. The lowest note is a mere accident of convenience. During the reign of the Lute it was common to vary the tuning of its strings according to the pitch of the song to be sung. Paganini, for certain pieces, altered the tuning of the strings of his Fiddle from the orthodox method, and Berlioz has directed the lowest string of the Double-bass to be altered in pitch for playing some of his works. The tuning, therefore, of an instrument, teaches us but little. The Japanese have an infinite number of modes of tuning, which, together with the occasional alteration of the bridges during the performance in order to obtain some lower notes, makes their free system seem arbitrary and very complicated to us.

14 [*Page* 115].—The answer to a fugue subject with us is not always strictly regular, so far as the exact intervals are concerned. The point to be aimed at is, to get the same motion of the notes comprising the phrase; it often happens that, without going out of the key, or introducing extraneous notes, the subject cannot always be repeated exactly spaced as it appeared in its initial setting forth.

15 [*Page* 123].—The examples which are given show that the Japanese have some acquaintance with harmony, and occasionally use it. The description of the classical "Form," and the analysis of the two pieces of Koto music given, will come as a surprise to most persons who look lightly on the music of this Eastern race. It is clear that they set forth a first and second subject, and that the form is what we know as the variation type; then their music displays imitative and sequential phrases, fanciful treatment of a simple recurrent theme, episodal passages, balanced sections; and the figures show considerable ingenuity in construction, even if we do not perceive any planned artistic effect. It would not be fair to place this music side by side with our own sonata form for the sake of comparison; but still their "Plum-branch" and "Rokudan," together with the graceful "On the Road to the Kasuga Temple," exhibit thought in construction and some distinct art-purpose. No doubt the large intervals employed in these pieces, and a prevalence of harsh intervals rarely used with us, make the music sound ungraceful to our ears; but the music is not without grace. As Dr. Hubert Parry has thoughtfully pointed out, our melodies are based on certain harmonic considerations; were the Japanese accustomed to hear our richly-harmonised themes, their ears would recognise certain laws which underlie the construction of melody itself, and their music would no doubt show the effect of this wider knowledge.

16 [*Page* 137].—It is to be regretted that nothing for certain is known of the ancient Hitsu-no-koto. It is reputed to have had as many as fifty strings, and it would supply a valuable piece of information if we only knew to what notes these strings were tuned. Speculation as to whether this large number of strings represented a diatonic or a chromatic scale-system is useless. But even if some of the notes were doubled—*i.e.*, two unisons—it is clear that the compass of this Harp, four thousand years old, must have been large, and its number of intervals very considerable.

17 [*Page* 137].—The striking of a stringed instrument with beaters or hammers is of great antiquity. Such instruments were the forerunners of our modern Dulcimer; the last lingering example is the Cembalo of the Hungarians, who play marvellously on this simply-constructed *piano-forte*, *i.e.*, an instrument yielding *soft* and *loud* tones according to the force with which the strings are struck. In many of the Assyrian sculptures will be found players with an instrument of this type suspended in front of them, while marching in procession with other musicians.

18 [*Page* 144].—The method of playing the one, two, and three-stringed Kin or Koto is curious, so far as the production of notes other than those of the open strings is concerned. It is difficult to say why, instead of stopping the string with the finger, as is common in all countries and with all instruments, a heavy ivory cylinder worn on the second finger of the left hand should have been employed: the sliding of this along the string, instead of striking it clear, has some little analogy to the action of our Violin and Violoncello players, who produce charming effects by this gliding up to a note. The indication of the position of the tones and semitones by spots painted on the body of the Koto is allied to the plan of using frets for a similar purpose placed across the necks of instruments of the Guitar type.

19 [*Page* 153].—This mode of raising the pitch of the string, by depressing that portion of it not intended to sound on the *wrong* side of the bridge, is an ingenious device peculiar to the Japanese musicians; so far as we know, the practice exists nowhere else, though it may be mentioned that the old Welsh harpists pinched their strings at the top in order to raise them a semitone. No one would guess that such a device was employed who merely *saw* the instrument. We should judge that the Koto possessed an imperfect scale: but this mode of artificially raising the pitch of a string by a single or a double pressure, either a semitone or a tone, elevates the instrument into the rank of one possessing a complete chromatic scale, and on it any music can be played.

20 [*Page* 153].—The device of sharpening a note from its initial pitch while the string is still vibrating, by tightening the tension of the string, and then, by gradually removing the pressure, letting the note fall to its original sound, is indeed remarkable; it suggests effects quite new to us. It may be pointed out, that some such result may be obtained by depressing still further the keys of the old Clavichord, *after* they have been struck and the tangents have hit the wire; the additional pressure on the key slightly raises, and thus tightens, the strings, making the note rise in pitch. There is a tradition that Bach, who preferred the Clavichord, used to produce this effect occasionally; but as the alteration of the pitch of a note would have affected the harmonic chord of which it was a component part, the tradition as to this after-sharpening seems hardly credible.

21 [*Page* 155].—The *Kaki* would seem to resemble in its effect our *acciaccatura*, which is a short grace-note lying beside and struck together with a longer principal note.

22 [*Page* 157].—The Japanese grace-notes and ornamentations, though not so numerous as our own, are of the same conventional and stereotyped character as those employed by the Harpsichord and Clavichord writers of the seventeenth and eighteenth centuries. But there is one special feature they use, the "Glissades," not found in our music. On instruments of the Pianoforte tribe, a *glissando* is possible only on the white notes forming the key of C; on the Harp, by means of its pedals setting the strings in any key required, the *glissando* can be

played just where desired; the ease with which it can be done has been a temptation to the Harpist to use the device so constantly that we find the expression "to sweep the strings" employed very often by the old writers of poetry. But it should be noted that the Harp and Pianoforte *glissando* necessarily took in every note of the diatonic scale; the Japanese, owing to the fact that there is no separate string for every note of the scale, omit certain notes in the *glissade*, and thus an effect is produced novel to our ears. The occasional introduction of this device in their pieces, the *glissade* being played both up and down *pianissimo*, lends a singular charm and romance to their music, besides affording a distinct contrast in tone-colour to the strings plucked with the plectrum.

23 [*Page* 159].—It is interesting to note the many refinements employed by the Japanese in the way in which the strings are plucked, sometimes with the plectrum, and sometimes the fingers, a difference being made (as by the players on our bow instruments) between the up and down-strokes of the exciting medium.

24 [*Page* 160].—"Uch.." This beating of the strings below the bridges is novel, and must produce an effect altogether strange to us.

25 [*Page* 160].—The Japanese notation is very interesting. It differs vastly from our own, than which we can think of nothing more exact or simple; yet it is complete enough to represent the time, the accent, the notes to be played, and the way in which the strings are to be plucked. It would be useful to have some historical account of the inception and gradual development of this system of notation.

26 [*Page* 166].—It would seem by this device that the strings are not so much stopped—as we use the term—as they are tightened by the varying pressure of the fingers, and so several notes can be produced by the finger in one position; the task must be a difficult one to do accurately.

27 [*Page* 171].—The omission of the fourth and seventh of the scale goes to show the great antiquity of the instrument, and that its series of sounds were of the pentatonic order, the most ancient type of the scale-systems.

28 [*Page* 172].—It would be incorrect to consider the vibrating wire in the body of the Gek-kin, Gen-kan, and Shigen, as an attempt to obtain sympathetic effects, as in the Viol d'Amour; there appears to be no tuning of this wire, and it could only produce a jangling effect.

29 [*Page* 175].—The use of snake-skin is an example of the custom which obtains of nations employing in the making of their musical instruments just such materials as are commonly found in their several countries. For instance, in European countries pine and maple are the woods chiefly selected for the bowed instruments, and until later times boxwood was employed for the wind instruments. In Egypt, the stems of the large reed plant, *Arundo donax*, form the flutes; in India, cane and gourds are made use of; in Siam, ivory; in China and Japan, bamboo; and in countries where snakes are common, the skins of these reptiles are pressed into use for musical purposes: Drums in Africa are often covered with the skins of lions. In Japan, the use of monkey-bone for the ancient Flute finds its parallelism in ancient Greece and Italy, where the early flute was made of the *tibia* bone, and this supplied the generic name for the whole family of instruments of this type. In Japan, as may be expected, a great deal of lacquer-work is employed with their instruments.

30 [*Page* 177].—It may be remarked that, provided the bridge is slightly rounded, the same effect of strings sounding together was produced on the old Italian "Accordo," by the hair of the bow being kept very loose, thus setting in vibration all the strings over which it passed.

31 [*Page* 181].—This peculiarity of a hole in the side of the Flute covered with paper is no doubt borrowed from the well-known Chinese type. Its effect is to create a *tremolo* by the rapid movements of the paper, which practically acts as a vibrating reed, and causes a distinct alteration in the character of the tone the tube gives out without this contrivance.

32 [*Page* 182].—In that the Hichiriki is played through a reed mouthpiece (*shita*) it should be more correctly classed with the reed (Oboe, Clarinet, and Bassoon) type of wind instrument, and not with the Flute proper, or the flue-organ-pipe type of tubed instruments.

33 [*Page* 183].—The Shakuhachi is of exactly the same character as the ancient long Flutes blown at the end, which are often seen in the Egyptian tomb paintings. The instrument (Nay) is still in use in the land of the Pharaohs; it is difficult to blow, the tone is singularly sweet and mellow.

34 [*Page* 185].—The Shō (Chinese "Cheng") is to us the most interesting of all Eastern instruments. Considering its elaborate construction, it is difficult to accept the statement made as to its enormous antiquity; yet it seems to have been known in China and Japan for centuries. The vibrating reed employed is that technically called the "single reed." No instrument of this character is known in Europe, but the Regal of the Middle Ages, occasionally used in place of the Organ in churches, and sometimes used in processions, as may be seen in some old pictures, was of this type so far as the tone was concerned. The sound was produced from the vibration of small reeds set in short pieces of pipe; but a bellows was employed to supply the wind, and the valves were opened from an ordinary key-board. The present representatives of the Regal are the Harmonium and the so-called American Organ. There is a tradition that the free reed came to us from China, but its principle has been known for thousands of years. Reeds were used for one of the species of the Greek αὐλός. It may be noted that the word in John, c. xii., v. 6, translated *bag* ("Judas was a thief, and had the bag"), is in the Greek version γλωσσόκ μον, *i.e.*, a box to keep the tongues or reeds in, just as modern Oboe, Clarinet, and Bassoon players still have to hold their reeds. The fact that several notes can be sounded at once on the Shō is sufficient to prove that the Japanese were at an early period of their history acquainted with harmony, *i.e.*, different notes sounded simultaneously. It is curious to note that instead of blowing into the pipes as we do, the Japanese draw in the breath, so the sound is produced by exhaustion of the air, and not by pressure of the breath; and, further, that we uncover the holes of our wind instruments with our fingers to produce the sound, whereas the Japanese in this instrument cover them—the reverse of our plan.

35 [*Page* 192].—It seems that in Japan, as in other Eastern countries, the Drum is regarded chiefly as an instrument of percussion to mark the time and accentuate the rhythm, the drummer having the same office as was assigned to the Coryphæus in the Greek orchestra; this official had a heavy metal shoe on his foot, and beat time by stamping on the stage. With us the Drum is much more extensively employed; indeed, Beethoven has elevated it into the rank of a solo instrument (*vide* "The Violin Concerto" and "The Choral Symphony").

36 [*Page* 211].—This shaking Drum, or Rattle, resembles the Sistrum of ancient Egypt. The instrument was deemed sacred; it consisted of a handle to which was attached a metal frame, and through the sides of this were thin metal bars moving to and fro when shaken. Sometimes pierced coins were strung on the bars to increase the jingle.

Of the various percussive instruments—and, indeed, of some of other types—it may be remarked how much more pains the Japanese seem to take in ornamenting them, and showing more feeling for art in their construction and ornamentation than is generally the case among the Western nations. The use of and fondness for colour is always more strongly shown in the East than in the West, and the musical instruments of these nations are beautifully painted, lacquered, and inlaid.

INDEX.

H.

I.

J.

2 G

T.

www.ingramcontent.com/pod-product-compliance
Lightning Source LLC
Chambersburg PA
CBHW030342270326
41926CB00009B/924